THE EMOTIONALLY INTELLIGENT INVESTOR

HOW SELF-AWARENESS, EMPATHY AND INTUITION DRIVE PERFORMANCE

RAVEE MEHTA

Pre-publishing technical and editorial assistance provided by LOTONtech at www.publishingdiy.co.uk.

For my parents and wife for their love and support

Table of Contents

Acknowledgements

Many were involved in making this book a reality.

My wife, Kate, was a constant source of encouragement.

Many mentors throughout my career were instrumental in my development as an investor. Michael Karsch was the most important mentor I had. I would also like to take this opportunity to thank Robert Soros, Bob Bishop, Robert Kim, Kristopher Segerberg, Frank Sica, Neal Moszkowski, David Wassong, Christian Michalik, Michael Pruzan, Suneel Kaji, Ari Benacerraf, OhSang Kwon and David Tayeh.

My editor, Tony Loton, himself a trading and investment author, provided necessary criticism and helped with the book's structure and layout.

I took inspiration for the title and styling of this book from the classic text *The Intelligent Investor* by Benjamin Graham – a veritable giant of the investing world. As Sir Isaac Newton might have said (paraphrased), "By standing on the shoulders of a giant, I hope to have seen further."

Finally, I would like to thank my family and friends, for their comments and review of the manuscript. I especially would like thank Christine Padlan for her valuable input.

About the Author

Ravee Mehta is a self-employed investor. Prior to managing his own money, Ravee was a managing director for eight years at Karsch Capital Management, LLC – a multibillion dollar hedge fund. At Karsch Capital, Ravee was responsible for evaluating long / short investment opportunities within the Technology and Telecommunications sectors globally. He previously held positions at Soros Fund Management LLC and Donaldson, Lufkin & Jenrette. Ravee graduated *summa cum laude*  from the University of Pennsylvania with degrees from both the Wharton School of Business and the School of Engineering and Applied Science. He has traveled in over 50 countries across six continents and lives in New York City with his wife Kate and dog Dixon.

You can find Ravee's companion web site for this book at:

www.theemotionallyintelligentinvestor.com.

"Like" the book on Facebook at:

www.facebook.com/TheEmotionallyIntelligentInvestor.

CHAPTER 1

Introduction

"I rely a great deal on *animal instincts*." - George Soros, *Soros on Soros*

"Hear a story, analyze and buy aggressively if it *feels right*." – Julian Robertson, *Market Wizards*

"I do an enormous amount of trading, not necessarily just for the profit, but also because it opens up other opportunities. I get a chance to *smell* a lot of things." – Michael Steinhardt, *Market Wizards*

"We simply attempt to be *fearful* when others are greedy and to be greedy when others are fearful" – Warren Buffett

"You need a certain amount of intelligence, but it's wasted over a certain level. After that it's more about *intuition*." – Stanley Druckenmiller

"You always want to know where the market is – whether it is *hot and excitable, or cold and stagnant*." – Bruce Kovner, *Market Wizards*

"We *don't* have an analytical advantage; we just look in the right place." – Seth Klarman

Kirk or Spock? Which Star Trek character would have been the better investor? According to most investing text books, the answer is easy. It would have been Spock. He was able to block out his emotions and make purely rational decisions. Yet, *none* of the great investors quoted above sounds like a highly logical Vulcan. The world's legendary money managers *use* their feelings. Instead of suppressing emotion, they actively sense what others in the market are thinking. They also employ gut instincts when making decisions. How is it possible that these great money managers complement rational thinking with some of their feelings to make better investment choices? How do they do so without being negatively influenced by those emotional biases that hurt everyone else? What exactly are these useful feelings? How can they be developed? How can they best be used? I decided that the answers to these questions were too important for me not to devote significant time to ponder and research them. Furthermore, since I could not find any one book that directly addressed all these questions, I decided the best way for me to learn, and hopefully help others, was to take on the challenge of writing one myself. This book is about trying to develop and utilize those types of intuitions and empathetic realizations that aid in successful investing. It is also about how to limit mistakes caused by those primal feelings, which can lead to biases that negatively impact returns.

The book is structured into three parts as follows.

PART 1 – Self-Awareness

Too many people try to emulate Warren Buffett even though they may have weaknesses, motivations and personality traits that are in conflict with his approach to investing. It would be like telling an aspiring basketball player who is only 5'8"to play like Shaquille O'Neal. The shorter player can still be great, but he needs to learn how to play in a different way. I used to work for George Soros, for example, and he would *never* have been successful if he used Buffett's style. Contrary to popular opinion, there does not seem to be one type of personality that is superior. The master investor adopts an approach for making decisions that bests fits with whom he or she is. Given this fact, it is amazing how little time most people actually spend on self-reflection. In Part 1, I provide a template for introspection and a framework for how one can develop an investment process that works best with one's unique set of attributes.

It is human nature to avoid feeling shame, regret and fear. In fact, we all create self-defense mechanisms against feeling these "negative" emotions. For example, some of us, me included, are vulnerable to realizing gains too quickly. Failing to sell a winner opens up the possibility of an eventual loss, which could make me feel regret or shame. Consequently, I often sell winning positions to avoid the risk of these negative feelings, even though it may be best to hold the investments longer. I consider this one of my weaknesses. Humans also use various mental shortcuts, especially when under stress. For example, stress often causes overtrading. When one is inordinately stressed, doing *something* feels better than doing nothing, even when the latter is more logical. Instead of actively reducing stress, most of us exacerbate the situation. We multitask. We operate under the assumption that we have an infinite capacity to digest information. We keep the TV on, talk on the phone and read emails and instant messages simultaneously. The brain does not operate best like this. In fact, research has demonstrated that our capacity for rational thought only allows for focusing on a relatively few things at once.

Our self-defense mechanisms, mental shortcuts and fluctuating moods cause common mistakes to occur when managing our investments. The initial stage of self-reflection should involve appreciating the specific problems to which you are most susceptible. These are your weaknesses. It is important to remember that people are different. Compared to me, you may be less likely to sell your winners too early. However, you may be more prone to other traps. The mistake most investment gurus make is to assume that you are like them. I illustrate some techniques to overcome each weakness, but no specific method works for everyone. There is no one-size-fits-all prescription. Each of us needs to conduct experimentation and self-reflection to recognize what works best.

Understanding personality traits and motivation is another important step before an investing style can be established. There are generally two ways to invest: one can either be contrarian, betting against the crowd, or one can bet that more investors will join the crowd and the current trend will continue. Each approach requires a different skill set, and certain personality traits influence how successful one can be when using each style. For example, a person that is impulsive and has high emotional sensitivity may find it more useful engaging an investing approach that bets on the current momentum continuing. He may also be better off utilizing stop-losses to limit the psychological pain from loss. Those with high emotional sensitivity often allow prior losses to negatively impact their future decision-making. On the other hand, siding with the current trend and employing stop-losses is inappropriate for an investor like Warren Buffett. Buffett is more thorough in his analysis and can maintain his emotional equilibrium, even after experiencing significant loss. Moreover, whether one is a short term trader or a longer term investor should be influenced by one's motivations. For example, people like Buffett, who enjoy learning about businesses' sustainable competitive advantages, are better off being longer term investors. Others, like Soros, who view investing as a vehicle for testing theories, should be open to a shorter term investing horizon. I conclude Part 1 by providing some techniques psychologists and investors utilize to continuously enhance their own self-awareness.

PART 2 – Social Awareness

Once we can understand the common mistakes people make simply because of human nature, we can then learn how to profit from their errors. This is where empathy comes in. In Part 2, I discuss how to use social awareness to get an edge. Our brains have something like a Wi-Fi network that can tap into the emotions of others. It is a terrible waste of mental resources not to put this powerful capability to use when investing. The ability to be in the shoes of other investors and feel what they are feeling is an indispensable weapon in the investor's armory. Paul Tudor Jones affirms that it is less important to understand news than to anticipate the market's reaction to it. The best way to do so is through empathy. For example, in early 1990, Jones empathized with the tremendous pressure Japanese fund managers were under to return at least 8% per year. While it may seem like an aggressive expectation in today's market, the average Japanese household in 1990 had become accustomed to making at least 8% per year. Any manager who underperformed that hurdle rate ran the risk of losing his job. So when the market sold off 4% in January, the Japanese portfolio managers had a choice: they could keep their jobs and still make the 8% minimum return by reallocating aggressively into bonds or they could take a risk on trying to outperform by buying even more equities. By putting himself in the shoes of the average Japanese fund manager, Jones realized that most of them would not want to risk their jobs. Consequently, Jones correctly bet that the Japanese stock market would suffer a major correction.[1]

Many investors use technical analysis but do not understand its significance. They think it is helpful, but they don't really understand *why*. Others compare chartists to astrologers. I used to be in the latter camp, but I will explain what convinced me to switch sides. A chart can evince a tremendous amount about what the current holders of a security may be *feeling*. Therefore, it can be helpful in developing an investing edge. I illustrate how ten of the most common chart reading principles can be explained using empathy. For example, a support level on a stock chart is the result of our bias to sell winners too early and our inclination to make associations with prior positive outcomes. Imagine several people, who originally bought IBM near $160 and sold it at $180. They each experienced a positive outcome. Most of these people will create a mental shortcut that associates buying IBM around $160 with a positive feeling. Therefore, $160 becomes a support level. In fact, this association can be so powerful that they can ignore facts such as a deteriorating outlook for the company's fundamentals or negative changes in the economy. Likewise, a resistance level on a stock chart is the result of the human self-defense mechanism against feeling the shame of being wrong. A resistance level is created when there are many holders anxiously waiting to sell for a lucky escape once they get back to a price that would yield a 'break-even' result or a slight gain. Imagine many people, who bought shares of Research in Motion (RIMM) at $15 because they were hopeful the company would turn its business around with new product introductions. After RIMM's new products got bad reviews, some of these people sold, causing the stock to drop sharply. Those who didn't exit, likely now feel stuck. They desperately want to avoid the shame that comes from selling at a loss, so they continue holding on to losing positions. They hope for a bounce back to $15, so that they can exit and break-even. Thus, $15 becomes a resistance level. In addition to explaining why the concepts of support and resistance make sense, I address several other chart reading ideas such as *why* a bull market tends to top out when the "leading" group of stocks starts underperforming or when there are fewer stocks making new highs.

We can also learn to use our own emotions to understand how others in similar circumstances may be feeling. For example, some investors use their own feeling of fear to know when a good time to buy is. If we need certain events to occur before being comfortable in an investment, others are probably feeling the same way. Consequently, we may want to take a chance and invest ahead of the events, especially if the stock's chart indicates a fair amount of support that is relatively close.

Finally, social awareness can lead to an edge when observing management speak or even when just reading an annual report. We are all dependent upon the top management of the companies we invest in. They are making investments with our money every day; therefore, we want to make sure that they are also self-aware. We also want to make sure that they are trustworthy. When interviewing management teams, we should challenge them to admit their true motivations and weaknesses. I suggest a process for how to be on the lookout for statements from management teams that imply that they lack self-examination or integrity.

PART 3 – Intuition

In part 3, I discuss how we can effectively develop and use intuition. Intuition is not some sort of magical sixth sense. Instead, it is a complex feeling that arises from pattern recognition. Chess grandmasters usually know their next move within a few seconds. Instead of suppressing their emotions, they first utilize gut feelings regarding their best possible move depending on how the pieces are laid out on the board. These grandmasters then use their reason to make sure the move is safe. If the initial gut instinct is found to be flawed, they start the cycle again with another intuitive feeling.[2] Many of the best investors seem to do something similar. For example, Warren Buffett does not start his investment process by comparing a bunch of possible investment alternatives. He does not depend on quantitative screening tools. Instead, Buffett intuitively gravitates towards a company he finds interesting and understands. He then analyzes the company, its industry, and its valuation to determine if the investment makes sense. If it does not, he moves on to the next company his intuition leads him to analyze. If the potential investment seems safe or attractive, Buffett refers back again to his intuition regarding the management's competency and trustworthiness. He also utilizes gut instincts with position sizing, overall market exposure, and in sensing danger.

Experience does not necessarily lead to expertise and intuition. In the same way chess grandmasters develop intuition through training exercises and reviewing prior matches, investors can use visualization exercises and certain techniques to make sure they get the most out of their experiences. By imagining certain situations and how you would react to them, you can build expertise without actually having to risk capital and significant time. Furthermore, with real-life experience, it is imperative to have a process that continuously evaluates choices in an objective way. Instead of just calling decisions bad or good, we should focus on why we made the decisions. We can also learn to better leverage the experience of others. You know you are on the right track when you are regularly seeing patterns that you would not have recognized before. I go over how these intuitions arise and how we can try to listen to them in a secure way. Finally, I provide case studies based on my own experience, to exemplify how intuition can be developed and safely harnessed.

In the final chapter of the book, I try to put everything together. I offer a dozen possible procedural recommendations that may improve decision-making. For example, relatively few investment firms incorporate personality tests in their recruiting processes. This is surprising, since most funds market a unique investing approach to their clients. Investment funds will have a much better chance of sticking to their investment style and will have better cultural unity if they actively recruit people with personality traits that best fit with their specific investment approaches. Moreover, in many firms, junior analysts, who have the least experience, are the employees most responsible for selecting ideas to work on. Junior analysts are also often relied upon for position sizing recommendations. Since idea selection and position sizing are two aspects of investing that most rely on intuition, this bottoms-up type process is nonsensical. It is an example of how intuition is often taken for granted. Senior members of an organization regularly assume that subordinates can recognize complex patterns as well as they can. I also briefly address what this book's concepts imply for non-professional individual investors and for clients of investment funds. Lastly, I mention how some of the ideas presented can influence life outside of investing.

Reflections on Myself

After eight years as a managing director at a well-respected hedge fund and at an age that is normally the peak of one's career on Wall Street, I made a somewhat controversial decision. I decided to quit my well-paying job to a take a step back to reflect. I traveled around the world, volunteered as a teacher in Western Africa and took a philosophy course at Oxford. After all these experiences and considerable reflection, I returned to New York with a reinvigorated passion for investing. I subsequently attempted to construct a system I could use to continuously improve. Writing this book is part of my journey in developing that framework. I plan to use it as a reference for the rest of my career.

Most acknowledge that investing is part art and part science. After studying both engineering and finance in school, I started my career with a pretty good handle on the scientific or analytical side. Therefore, I understood that if I wanted to grow into a superior investor, I needed to better know the "art" of investing. While there is a plethora of books that addresses analytic decision-making with respect to financial decisions, I had difficulty finding much out there about the less scientific side of investing. There are various aspects of the artistic side, but the focus for this book is how we can better employ our emotional brain processes to make more profitable investment decisions. I'll save other aspects, such as creativity, for another time or for another writer.

Investing Philosophy and Psychology

Since Plato, people have been preaching suppression of emotions in favor of rationality. Plato believed that the soul was constantly torn between reason and impulsive emotion and that we needed to try to tame the "beast inside of us" to make the best decisions in life. This line of reasoning was somewhat supported by a popular 2005 *Wall Street Journal* article titled, "Lessons from the Brain-Damaged Investor." Research had been done on people that had damage in one or more parts of the brain that generate emotions. Participants were given $20 to start and were told that they would have to make a series of "invest or not invest" decisions before 20 coin flips. If they decided to invest and the coin landed on heads they would lose $1.00. If it landed on tails the subjects would receive $2.50. After the experiment, they could take home whatever they had accumulated. The expected outcome of each round was +$0.75. Therefore, the most optimal decision was to invest in every chance. The study found that these brain damaged patients were more likely to do just that. Many people in the control group were not as logical. After losing a prior round, a significant portion of the 'normal' group started to fear loss and this resulted in excessive risk aversion.[3] I remember wondering why Wall Street was not full of people that had brain damage. Since I was having a good year at the time, I even wondered if I needed to get myself checked out! It turns out that while these brain-damaged patients may do well in a very simple experiment like this, they do poorly with investments in real-life. The real world is characterized by many variables, scarce information and time constraints. Although many of these patients could be highly intelligent, they wind up unable to make everyday decisions like what to wear in the morning, where to park and where to eat. They tend to endlessly deliberate the pros and cons of every small decision.[4] Given all the decisions we need to make every day, it is impossible to appropriately analyze every one of them. Other similarly brain-damaged patients have been shown to make overly risky decisions. We *need* to feel fear in order to avoid taking excessive risk.[5] In *The Social Animal*, David Brooks summarizes a key finding of recent research of the brain. Brooks affirms, "Reason and emotion are not separate and opposed. Reason is nestled upon emotion and dependent upon it. Emotion assigns value to things, and reason can only make choices on the basis of those valuations."[6]

The brain is designed in such a way that optimal decision-making is intertwined with emotion. In a cross-disciplinary project, John Ameriks, Tanja Wranik, and Peter Salovey conducted a study of 2,595 Vanguard IRA and 401k investors in 2005 and 2006. They asked each participant to complete psychological tests that measured aspects of their emotional intelligence and personality then monitored their investment decisions. They defined emotional intelligence as four competencies that involve perceiving, using, understanding and managing emotions and scored each of these aptitudes separately for each subject. People ranking high in 'perceiving' easily recognize emotional signals in others. They are more empathetic. Those who score well in 'using' employ their feelings more when making decisions. They are the type of people who do not do something, because it feels "wrong." Participants highly ranked in 'understanding' are good in articulating how they feel. Finally, those who score well in 'managing' are great at regulating their emotions. Plato would probably have scored highly in 'managing', for example. According to the theory that it is best to be rational by suppressing emotion, one would expect that investors who could better manage their emotions would be the ones who perform best. In fact, the participants that scored highest in their ability to *use* their emotions were the superior investors! The next best performance was from the subjects that scored highest in *perceiving* emotions. The ability to manage one's emotions appeared to be the least important competency of one's emotional intelligence.[7] The team demonstrated that we need to do much more than just keep our feelings in check; we need to actually utilize our feelings to make the best decisions. While the researchers had no way of confirming what emotions the best investors were using, I hypothesize that it was a combination of intuitive and empathetic feelings that led to conviction in their decisions. A great thing is that all of us can become better at using and perceiving emotions. Unlike IQ and most personality traits, which are relatively fixed after our early teenage years, research has proven that our emotional intelligence can be strengthened with effort.[8]

Investment firms are increasingly pressured to be more transparent about their decision processes, for various reasons that range from the fallout of the Madoff Ponzi scheme and higher regulatory scrutiny to greater employee hierarchy. While the increased transparency may satisfy clients or regulators and may allow for better management of organizations with growing headcounts, it also comes at a considerable cost: less use of intuition and social awareness and over-use of rational / analytical thought processes. More often than not, when financial analysts are forced to write detailed memos regarding their ideas and trading recommendations, they abandon their intuitions and overly focus on quantitative or more analytical aspects of the investment. This can inevitably lead to an overly low tolerance for uncertainty, incorrect position sizing, frustration between the portfolio manager and analysts and other issues that result in suboptimal performance. Moreover, computer programs now account for the majority of the daily volume on most stock exchanges. If we are going to outsmart the computers and other human players in the market, we will increasingly need to harness some of our emotional thought processes more effectively. Feelings are our main competitive advantage against the machines and ever more against humans who are increasingly suppressing their intuitions.

Professional investors sometimes talk about high conviction trades similarly to how professional basketball players talk about being "in the zone". A basketball player in the zone has a strong feeling that his shot will go into the basket before it even leaves his hands. Similarly, a professional investor, who feels high conviction in a trade, intuitively knows that the probability of success is high. The decision just *feels* right! Professional investors are trained to be aggressive with position sizing whenever this strong feeling arises. The problem is that for most of us, high conviction in an investment decision is rare. Maybe a better understanding of what this feeling actually is will increase the chances of feeling it? The Merriam-Webster online dictionary defines conviction as "a strong persuasion or belief", but what makes a belief in an investment idea "strong"? After reflecting on my own high conviction trades over the past several years, I affirm that conviction is developed not just by using feelings, nor just by rationality, but by the two sides of the brain being in sync. Conviction is arrived at through the recognition of patterns that remind the investor of previous successes. What seems uncertain to most, is relatively predictable to the investor with high conviction. But that is not enough. Conviction also requires analytically and comprehensively understanding the fundamentals of the company and the industry one is investing in. It involves a good understanding of the emotions of the current holders of the security, and an appreciation of what other investors looking at the stock may or may not do if certain events occur. High conviction is not overconfidence. Overconfident investors are not prepared for what can go wrong. An investor making a high conviction trade is quick to recognize when to be even more aggressive and is equally fast to sense danger and get out.

There are many books on how one can better rationally analyze investment options. In this book, I focus on the more "touchy-feely" aspects of conviction. Many investors and traders are the type of people that are scared off by words like "self-reflection" and "empathy". If you are one of those people, this book is vital for you. Hopefully, after reading it, you will, like me, develop a much better understanding of yourself and how you can utilize empathy and intuition to make a better percentage of high conviction decisions that lead to improved returns both for your portfolio and your general well-being. I view investing as an instrument for overall self-improvement. Dr. Brett Steenbarger, a psychologist and trader, writes, "Every gain is an opportunity to overcome greed and overconfidence. Every loss is an opportunity to build resilience."[9] Each decision is a chance to learn something valuable about myself. Cultivating self-awareness, empathy and intuition in a way that is supplemented with rational thinking does more than empower someone striving to reach his or her potential as an investor. These things also help one become a better person and live a more fulfilling life. That realization is what made me understand that I loved investing.

What You Might Want to Ask Before We Start

In the spirit of being empathetic, I have tried to anticipate a few initial questions you may have, and I have answered them:

Why should I listen to you?

It's fair to ask what qualifies me to explore self-awareness, empathy and intuition with respect to investing. While I graduated *summa cum laude* from The Wharton School of Business and simultaneously completed an engineering degree, I have never published anything before and I am not a psychologist or an economist. I worked at a couple of respected multi-billion dollar hedge funds – Soros Fund

Management and Karsch Capital Management. While in school, I worked odd jobs and incurred massive debt in order to pay tuition. I am now in the fortunate position of not needing to work for anyone else. However, I am certainly much less successful than many other professional investors, especially when compared to those I reference. I was also probably lucky to have entered the hedge fund industry when I did. As I related earlier, the purpose of writing this book is to help *me* become a better investor. If it helps others, that would constitute as a bonus. The book is a compilation of (i) research I have read from prominent academics that specialize in decision-making, (ii) reflections on my past mistakes (of which there are many!) and successes, (iii) lessons from various mentors throughout my career, and (iv) the study of some of the statistically better decision-makers in the investment management industry. I have personal relationships with portfolio managers and analysts at many of the world's largest hedge funds and have also tried to learn from their respective firms' best practice approaches.

For whom is the book intended?

The book is primarily written for professionals working at investment management firms. However, the material discussed is purposely kept relatively simple so that the individual non-professional investor can also benefit. I show how professional investors have several advantages despite the government's effort to level the playing field. Additionally, I demonstrate how individual private investors can play to their strengths and (in some cases) outwit the professionals. Clients of investment funds may also learn how to better evaluate those who manage their assets.

The concepts in this book are applicable to both longer term investors and shorter term traders. After all, both types of money managers are doing the same thing at a high level. They both buy with the anticipation of generating an acceptable return. In fact, one of the main points I make in the book is that it is premature to decide on an investing style without first understanding oneself. While I consider a "trader" anyone who has an investment timeframe of less than a year, I describe all types of money managers as "investors."

I invite the reader to join me on this journey. I hope it will prove helpful in a time when the analytical side of investing seems to be much more in vogue.

So many great investors have talked about how the secret to their success is discipline. Are you disagreeing with them?

Not at all! Discipline is certainly required to safeguard against many of the common investing traps that are caused by our desire to avoid feeling negative emotions and stress. However, even the investors who preach self-discipline need to ultimately rely on their emotions to make investments. Warren Buffett did not have a mathematical formula to help him decide that GEICO would be a great purchase. Even if he had a formula, how did he decide to spend time understanding GEICO instead of all the other companies out there? How does Buffett decide to invest $1 billion into one company and only $100 million into another? How does he decide who the CEOs of his companies should be? How does Buffett appreciate that others are fearful enough for him to start being more greedy? The answers to all of these questions and others like them depend upon intuition and empathy. It is therefore wrong to ignore all feelings, since intuition and empathy are based on emotion. Buffett sticks to an approach that works well with his weaknesses, motivations and personality traits. His does not ignore emotions. Rather, Buffett relies heavily upon them. His discipline enables him to utilize his intuitive and empathetic feelings in a safe manner. This book offers a framework for self-reflection so that people can develop an investment strategy that fits their unique behavioral characteristics and motivations. Once a strategy is developed, it is vital to be disciplined. Experience does not necessarily lead to intuition. Thus, it is necessary to have a methodical process that enables one to get the most out of experience. While I focus on self-awareness, empathy and intuition in this book, I obviously still think traditional analysis is extremely important. Just like the chess grandmaster, an investor should be guided by intuition, but the majority of his time should be spent on logical reasoning to make sure his gut instincts are in check. Therefore, my goal is to optimally complement fundamental analysis. I do not mean to belittle it in any way.

Isn't the stock market too complex for intuition?

In *The Power of Intuition*, Gary Klein, who has been researching decision-making for decades, cites how a large percentage of mutual funds consistently underperform the market indices. To him, this is proof that intuitions built from investing experience do not translate into better decision-making.[10] The psychologist Daniel Kahneman, a Nobel laureate, also affirms that the stock market is too complex and random for helpful gut instincts to develop. Furthermore, if intuition comes from experience, critics argue that we should theoretically see investment performance improve with age. This does not seem to be the case as many great investors such as Michael Steinhardt, who often mentioned the importance of instinct, perform worse in their later years. These arguments are flawed. While the overall market may seem complex and random, I will show how there are many patterns within it that recur frequently. The best money managers recognize patterns developing ahead of most. The intuitive decision-making that is involved with investing is much more complicated than other types of decision-making. However, that does not mean that we should abandon trying to better develop and use gut instincts when we invest. While it is true that most mutual funds underperform, a small percentage outperform consistently, which suggests that there is a handful of investors with a superior approach.[11] Without a good investment strategy, primal emotions of regret and fear can overwhelm helpful gut instincts. Many professional investors are either not self-aware enough to know how these emotions can impact them or they are trained to completely ignore all feelings along with their helpful intuitions. Most investors also do not recognize when good luck may have significantly impacted their trading performance. Consequently, they often develop gut instincts that are not helpful. Moreover, because other market participants are constantly on the lookout for successful strategies that can be back-tested, intuitions run the risk of going obsolete over time and the successful investor needs to be on the lookout for this obsolescence. Finally, for the short term trader, intuitive decision-making often involves the added complexity of needing to have gut instincts concerning other people's gut instincts. This can be a very challenging skill to maintain over a long period of time, especially since good performance usually leads to the accumulation of a greater amount of assets, which cannot be managed as dynamically as before.

Aren't many of these "great" investors you analyze just lucky?

Some may question the study of decision-making by the best investors. In *Fooled by Randomness*, Nassim Taleb argues that this is a dangerous exercise since many of the "best" investors are just lucky.[12] If 200 people flip a coin 11 times, 5 people are statistically likely to hit heads every time.[13] Taleb argues that studying successful investors is the same as studying those 5 lucky people in the set of 200. In a 1984 talk given at Columbia University, Warren Buffett disagreed with this line of thinking citing how many successful investors, such as himself, were trained similarly by Benjamin Graham. He said, "I think you will find that a disproportionate number of successful coin-flippers in the investment world came from a very small intellectual village."[14] This proved to Buffett that success could not just be random. While I agree with Buffett, Taleb makes an interesting point. Strong investment returns do not necessarily imply skill. I restricted my analysis to only those investors who had very long term track records of success in order to limit my chance of just analyzing a "lucky coin flipper."

PART 1
SELF-AWARENESS

CHAPTER 2

Why is Self-Awareness Important?

"You must know yourself if you want to accomplish anything in life." – Jim Rogers, *A Gift to My Children*

Warren Buffett is a great investor. However, if George Soros tried to be like Buffett, he would very likely have been a failure. Soros, like many of the best investors, is successful because he knows himself. He developed a strategy and investment style that fits with his specific set of motivations, strengths, weaknesses, and personality traits. Buffett enjoys learning how businesses operate and loves finding new businesses with sustainable competitive advantages. He likes to be a long term partner with management. On the other hand, Soros' motivation is derived from his love of philosophy. He views investing as a means for testing his theories.[15] Therefore, Soros does not necessarily have an investment time horizon. If he realizes he is incorrect, he may reverse his position the day after it is initiated. At the same time, Soros could be in the same investment for years, as long as his theory concerning it still proves valid. Buffett is cautious while Soros can be impulsive. Buffett has a lower tolerance for ambiguity than Soros. While Buffett walks away from any business he does not understand, Soros views uncertainty as part of the opportunity. Both investors are excellent in avoiding overconfidence, but they do so in different ways. Buffett utilizes a partner, maintains a humble lifestyle and is relatively even-keeled emotionally. Soros is constantly on the lookout for the flaws in his thesis and is highly open to the ideas of others. While his mood and emotions seem to fluctuate much more than Buffett's, Soros uses his relatively high self-awareness regarding his emotional and even physical states to his advantage. He sometimes changes his views at the onset of acute back pain, for example. Like Buffett and Soros, we each need to tailor our investment style to fit our own personal attributes and tendencies.

According to Dr. Travis Bradberry, who conducts research on organizational performance—"83% of those with high self-awareness are top performers". Likewise, just 2% of bottom performers are high in self-awareness."[16] His research concerns job functions across the entire economy and is not restricted to investment professionals. Nevertheless, the takeaway of his research is striking. Self-awareness appears to be more correlated with pay and success than IQ or any personality trait. Understanding your strengths, motivations and what types of situations impact your emotional equilibrium is the key to achievement—not only with investing, but also in practically any other endeavor. Furthermore, only if we are aware of what we are feeling can we distinguish helpful gut feelings from our biasing emotions. Despite the relatively high correlation between success and self-awareness, very few people actually focus on developing it. Bradberry states, "Only 36% of the people we tested are able to accurately identify their emotions as they happen. This means that two thirds of us are typically controlled by our emotions and are not yet skilled at spotting those feelings and using them to our benefit."[17]

Some may wonder if there is a certain "personality" that is better for an investor to have. Several researchers have studied this topic and have not found a trait that benefits investors over a long period of time. According to Dr. Richard Peterson, who specializes in researching emotion as it relates to financial decision-making, "It is true that individual personality traits are associated with investment success in different economic climates, but no one trait or combination of traits is consistently correlated with investment profits over time." For example, extroverted investors were found to do better in bull markets and introverts were found to do better in bear markets. Dr. Peterson also states, "It turns out knowing your personality propensities and understanding the conditions in which they predispose you to thrive are greater predictors of success than the traits themselves."[18]

The good news is that unlike personality traits (extroversion, conscientiousness, agreeableness, etc.) and IQ, which measures the ability to learn, emotional intelligence has been shown to significantly improve with effort. In fact, researchers have demonstrated that just thinking about self-awareness can result in progress. In *Emotional Intelligence 2.0*, Travis Bradberry, states, "The surprising thing about self-awareness is that just thinking about it helps you improve the skill, even though much of your focus initially tends to be on what you do 'wrong'." I will not take credit yet, but just by the fact that you have read this book to this point, you are already on your way to becoming more self-aware and therefore a better investor.

In the following chapter, I will discuss some of the emotional biases that negatively impact the investor that is not self-aware. One useful exercise is to keep a journal in which you try to keep track of when and how often you fall victim to these common mistakes as well as when you are successful in avoiding them. Using this and other techniques discussed throughout the book will help you to better understand your weaknesses and your strengths. If you have a tendency to fall victim to a common trap, consider it a weakness. If you are not susceptible to a specific trap, consider this aspect of yourself to be a strong point. In Chapter 4, I illustrate how some of the best investors deal with their own specific weaknesses. I also address other personal dimensions to consider such as motivation, personality traits and tolerance for uncertainty. Only after one is self-aware regarding these aspects, can one consider an investment approach.

An investment strategy should minimize mistakes to which you may be most susceptible and it should capitalize on your strengths. It should fit with your personality and your motivation. Once an approach is established, it is important to stay consistent. After going through this exercise myself, I believe I have developed an investing style that fits me. I cannot tell you what is exactly right for you. The purpose of the next few chapters is to provide a framework and some ideas for you to start your own process of self-reflection and then to consider an investment approach that will work best for you. I call it a process because it is something any good investor needs to constantly work on. Some of our personal attributes, such as our tolerance for ambiguity, can be quite dynamic. People who are self-aware are precisely that way because they make self-examination a routine part of their lives. This is too vital for success to be haphazard. There are many investors who just work on self-awareness after they experience painful losses. This usually results in a cycle where losses lead to better discipline, which yields better returns, which is followed by hubris, laziness and lack of self-reflection. Inevitably, the cycle repeats after the resulting poor performance. The fallout is investment returns and a quality of life that is significantly worse than its potential. For some, a down-cycle may result in losses so severe and scarring that they can be career-ending. A consistent approach to self-reflection is the key to breaking out of this common cycle and to achieving one's potential.

CHAPTER 3

Common Weaknesses

"I have made so many decisions and mistakes that it has made me wise beyond my years as an investor." – Michael Steinhardt, *Market Wizards*

Every investor has vulnerabilities and I am certainly no exception. In this section, I list some of the most common traps attributable to human nature. You will need to reflect on past mistakes to figure out to which ones you are most susceptible. I try to write a short entry in a trading journal every day. I briefly write about past mistakes and what I did well. I also try to keep track of missed opportunities and disasters that were avoided. I attempt to record what I am currently feeling, and how I felt when mistakes or good decisions were made (irrespective of whether those good or bad decisions led to good or bad results). I also visualize current investments going against me and how I would feel in those instances. During these mental simulations, I ask myself if I fell for one of the common traps or if I led with one of my strengths. A journal is just one tool for self-reflection. It may or may not be right for you, but the most important takeaway is that you need to try and find some way of objectively recognizing your vulnerabilities and strengths.

Our common investing mistakes can be placed into three categories:

- Self-defense mechanisms against feeling shame, regret and fear.
- Irrational reactions to stress and overloading of the brain's capacity for rational thought.
- Vulnerabilities caused by fluctuations in mood.

I describe some of the most common weaknesses across these three categories in this chapter. This is not a complete list. Moreover, behavioral economists are constantly finding new vulnerabilities that humans have with making optimal investment decisions.

Self-Defense Mechanisms Against Feeling Shame, Regret and Fear

This first grouping involves our self-defense mechanisms against feeling shame, regret and fear. As you will see, we are inclined to do many irrational things in our attempt to avoid these negative feelings.

Risk Aversion

We fear losing money much more than we enjoy making it. Daniel Kahneman states, "Given a choice between risky outcomes, human beings are twice as averse to losses as to comparable gains."[19] The most obvious self-defense mechanism against the fear of loss is to not take much risk. This is why many of the subjects without brain-damage in the coin tossing experiment described in Chapter 1 stopped betting, even though the expected outcome was positive. While our natural risk aversion is often beneficial, it can also lead to illogical decisions. For example, risk aversion is cited as one of the main reasons most young people over-allocate their investment portfolios towards safer fixed-income investments despite the fact that equities have been shown to outperform bonds over very long periods of time.

Holding Losers Too Long and Selling Winners Too Early

It is human nature to want to feel like we made the "right" decisions. Not being correct can lead to shame or shame's cousin — regret. This is a very difficult burden when investing, since even the best investors make many mistakes. Instead of letting ourselves feel shame or regret, many of us hold on to losing positions in a hope that we will be proven "right." People who fall for this trap also usually sell their winners too quickly. After all, the best way to prove you were "right" is to lock-in a gain. The risk of a small gain evaporating and therefore being "wrong" can carry a higher psychological penalty than the happiness from earning significantly more money on the investment. This bias is stronger when we come up with an investment idea ourselves. In other words, we are more likely to hold our winners longer and cut short our losses earlier when we get the investment idea from other people such as brokers or research analysts.

Taking Excess Risk After Losses

The psychological need to be "right" and avoid feeling shame and regret can be so powerful that we sometimes take increased risk when there is no logical reason to do so. Instead of reevaluating a losing investment with an open mind, some of us opt for mindlessly adding to the position to get our average cost lower. If you ever started recklessly betting a larger than normal amount in a casino to get back to "even," you should know what I am talking about. We can fall for this trap even if there are fundamental changes that justify our investments to have lost money. This bias can take another form, when one actually does exit a losing position only to take much more risk with future investments. We become motivated to get the entire portfolio back to "break-even" as quick as possible. As we grow up, we are inculcated with the idea that persistence pays off. Unfortunately, persistence in dollar cost averaging for its own sake can be dangerous with investing. To be clear, there is nothing wrong with adding to positions on weakness when fundamentals and your view of a company's intrinsic value have not changed. What is incorrect is adding to losers just for the sake of adding, so that you are not proven "wrong." Another way this bias evinces itself is when we take excess risk after losing something we *think* we were about to have. According to Charlie Munger in *The Psychology of Human Misjudgment*, which was brilliantly written at the age of 81, "If a man almost gets something he greatly wants and has it jerked away from him at the last moment, he will react much as if he had long owned the reward and had it jerked away."[20] Auctions such as those done on eBay take advantage of this bias. Some of us act quite irrationally when others begin to outbid us towards the end of the auction, or when we participate in future auctions for similar types of products.

Herding

In *Trading from Your Gut*, trader Curtis Faith states, "One of the mental shortcuts that our brains are programmed to make is the belief that doing what others are doing is safer than doing something different."[21] For most of us, envy plays a large role in determining success. The writer H. L. Mencken once jokingly related how success depends on making "at least $100 more a year than the income of one's wife's sister's husband."[22] We are much more inclined to feel sadness or shame when everyone around us is doing well and we are not. Consequently, in order to avoid feeling bad, we tend to just do what others do. We are compelled to join the herd. The German psychologist Gerd Gigerenzer argues that our propensity to be part of a group is so powerful that it can even override moral rules and can cause people who are ordinarily good to become killers.[23]

Anchoring

Yet another way people avoid feeling regret is by fixating on certain prices. For example, investors sometimes do not want to buy a stock that just went up 10% in the last week, even though they still think the stock is significantly undervalued. They regret not buying the stock a week ago and become fixated on the price that they missed. In the movie *Too Big to Fail*, Dick Fuld, the former CEO of Lehman Brothers, was portrayed several times as someone who fell for this psychological trap. Fuld anchored on his stock's 52-week high of $66 per share when negotiating with potential investors. He had a difficult time accepting a large discount to that fixated number, regardless of where the stock was trading at the time and despite the fact that a capital infusion was badly needed to save the firm. The movie depicted Fuld as a man who became very difficult for potential investors to deal with because of his anchoring bias. Many of us can also fall victim to this bias with the overall market. At times, I found myself to be much more constructive on the market. Nevertheless, I was reluctant to add significant exposure because I missed a recent large move. By the way, retailers have learned to take advantage of our anchoring bias. If you ever found yourself thinking you got a good deal relative to a "suggested" or pre-discounted price, you probably were anchoring.

Overly Focusing on Win / Loss Count

We can mentally avoid feeling shame and sadness by focusing on how many times we were "right" as opposed to "wrong", or how many days or months we made money. Of course, this is absurd. In investing, you can have many winners which can be more than offset by a single loser. Similarly, you can have lost money every day of the year except one and still have generated a positive return. A friend, who likes to sell options, recently was a victim of this mental trap. The vast majority of out-of-the-money options expire worthless, so selling them can produce a lot of winners. As the number of positive return days and number of winners went up, he felt ever more confident in selling more options. The problem was that the minority of options that did not expire worthless resulted in losses so severe that they wiped out all of my friend's gains over the past year in a single week.

Overconfidence

Rationalization and denial are two common mental self-defense mechanisms. When investing, they help us avoid feeling shame and sadness. Sometimes when we have invested much of our time, reputation and / or money into understanding and presenting the merits of an investment, we do not treat the invested time as a sunk cost. Instead, we let it impact how we interpret new data. We ignore news that goes against our thesis or we try to spin the news so that it seems supportive. In *Mental Strategies of Top Traders*, one of the anonymous SAC traders that trading coach Ari Kiev interviews says, "There seems to be this misconception in finance that the more work you do, the more likely you are to make money in a stock. In some cases, this is true. In a lot of cases, it's not only wrong, it's actually worse because you become overconfident."[24] Moreover, overconfidence leads to what psychologists call the "endowment effect," which is when we think our possessions are worth more than they objectively are. This is well apparent in residential real estate, where people attach to the value of a house their years of work to maintain it and even their positive memories of seeing their children grow up in it. They somehow think that the buyer will care and pay up for all those memories.[25] In the 2011 Berkshire annual meeting, Charlie Munger said that he and Warren Buffett do not rely much on financial projections. Munger related that when people put numbers in a spreadsheet, the projections tend to become more real than they really are. This is another example of the endowment effect. People can become overconfident in their own financial projections. It is much easier for an analyst to criticize the assumptions made by others than to find fault in his own financial forecasts.

Hindsight Bias

A close relative of the overconfidence bias is hindsight bias. It is another way we rationalize, so that we don't feel ashamed. In *The*

Black Swan, Nassim Taleb affirms that we regularly revise memories and even invent new ones.[26] We do this to prove that we were "right" all along even though our portfolios may be showing losses. Someone who suffers from hindsight bias tends to make claims such as "I told you I was becoming more bullish two months ago" even though he or she did not increase exposure to the market. Another example is when someone says "I knew Company XYZ was going bankrupt" even though he or she did not make a short sale on the company's stock to benefit from such insight. Not only does hindsight bias take the focus away from self-improvement, it also can be especially dangerous when combined with our bias to take excess risk after losses. If we feel like we really should have made more money, we may want to take excess risk with future investments in order to get back "even" to the net worth we believe we should have been at. Hindsight bias from a firm's leader can also lead to deterioration in culture as frustrated employees are repeatedly blamed for poor performance and for not "following their leader."

Status Quo Bias

In a chapter of *Emotional Intelligence in Everyday Life*, Peter Salovey, a psychology professor at Yale University, described an experiment where two different groups were given an inheritance. They were told to decide on how they should invest the money among a set of investment options (high risk equities, municipal bonds, treasury bills, etc.). One group was just given cash, whereas the second group was given an existing portfolio already primarily invested in one asset class. The vast majority of the people in the second group kept the high allocation to the specific asset class unchanged. The experiment confirmed that once we have a portfolio, we are unlikely to make many changes. This bias occurs even when we inherit a portfolio from someone else.[27] Again, the status quo bias is a result of our relentless desire to avoid shame. The psychological risk of doing something and being "wrong" can be greater than our perceived reward of making a change and being "right."

Externalization

A common self-defense mechanism is to blame factors outside your control. By blaming losses on influences like the market's volatility, the Federal Reserve, or the German parliament, people attempt to avoid feeling shame for their own actions. While losses may very well be the result of unanticipated factors, it is imperative to constantly put the focus on what can be controlled. Otherwise, improvement will never come. Furthermore, people who feel like they are in control generally feel less fear. Therefore, regularly blaming outside factors for poor performance can exacerbate risk aversion, herding and other biases. It increases the psychological need we feel to defend ourselves.

Irrational Reactions to Stress and Overloading of the Brain's Capacity for Rational Thought

The second category of mistakes involves our reaction to stress and what happens when we overload our capacity for rational thought. The brain's pre-frontal cortex, which is the area most associated with rational thought, can easily be weighed down with too much information or can be starved of oxygen and nutrients when stress causes other brain centers to consume resources that it would otherwise get. Our natural response is to use mental shortcuts that reduce the load on our rational brain regions. These shortcuts may be useful in many areas of life, but can be disastrous with investing.

Overtrading

When we are overly stressed or scared, our natural reaction is to want to do something. Scientists describe this as the "fight or flight" response, and it can lead to overtrading. Making trades is a way of doing something. When you are inordinately stressed, doing *something* often feels better than doing nothing. Paul Andreassen at Harvard University conducted an experiment on two sets of subjects managing identical portfolios. The first group was told to watch certain financial programs and read articles pertaining to their investments. The other group was told to not digest any financial media. The group that received less information did significantly better than the other group. What was particularly interesting was that the nature of the news didn't seem to matter. Even if the first group only read positive news articles about its holdings, it would still have done worse.[28] Increased information caused stress, which resulted in overtrading. While the "fight or flight" response may be beneficial in some situations in life, doing nothing impulsive is usually the best course of action when investing. Warren Buffett uses a baseball analogy to make this point. Buffett writes, "To be a good hitter, you've got to get a good ball to hit. It's the first rule in the book. If I have to bite at stuff that is out of my happy zone, I'm not a .344 hitter. I might only be a .250 hitter."[29] Our investment decisions will be terrible if they are motivated by stress relief.

Too Much Noise / Information

Not only can too much information result in higher stress, it can also overload our brain's capacity for analysis. The brain's rational processing centers, such as the pre-frontal cortex, can only handle so much information at one time. Too many variables can cause us to forget about what is important. Psychologists at the University of Amsterdam have demonstrated this phenomenon through several experiments. In one such experiment, two groups of subjects were given ratings regarding features of four different automobiles. The experiment was set up so that one car should clearly stand out as being the best. The first group was given ratings for four important features for each car. The second group was given ratings across twelve different categories. Conventional wisdom would imply that the group with more information would be better able to pick the best car. The opposite was found to be true. The second group wound up actually doing even worse than random chance – they picked the best car less than 25% of the time, while most in the first group picked correctly.[30] Increasing the number of variables under consideration overloaded most people's ability to think rationally. When digesting a lot of information, we need to make sure we have enough time to appropriately understand what is most important. Multitasking has also been shown to negatively impact rational thinking. As smart as we think we are, our rational brain capacity is limited and can easily be overburdened by either doing too many things at once or by focusing on every data point, no matter how irrelevant.

Overlooking Very Low Probability Events

Another mental shortcut is to spend very little time thinking about low probability events. What are the chances of another Dust Bowl occurring in the Midwest or of a tsunami hitting New York City? The probabilities are so low that we do not feel the need to factor them into our analysis. This is a reasonable way to live our lives. After all, if we truly contemplated all the low probability things that could happen to us, we wouldn't have time to do anything else. Furthermore, in a diversified portfolio, the losses that arise from negative company-specific low probability events should be absorbable. The problem is when we oversimplify to a degree that ignores how certain large scale low probability events can impact our entire portfolio at the same time. Nassim Taleb has shown how oversimplification has regularly caused people to undervalue insurance that would protect their portfolios against "Black Swan" type risks.[31]

Recency Bias

While investors tend to underestimate the impact of low probability events to their portfolios, they also are inclined to overestimate the probability of events that recently occurred. For example, after the tsunami hit Japan in 2011, investors became much more concerned about future tsunamis. If your neighborhood is flooded for the first time in 100 years, you will likely pay a premium for flood insurance even though the probability of another flood remains very low. Similarly, if the management team of the last company you invested in made a controversial acquisition that caused the stock to go down, you may tend to avoid any acquisitive companies for your next investment. As these examples illustrate, recency bias is an oversimplification that can result in irrational decision-making.

Association Shortcut

Another common mental shortcut is to associate prior positive outcomes to current situations. For example, if we realized a gain on a specific stock, we are inclined to buy it back if it gets back close to the same price we originally bought it at. Even if the company's fundamentals may have negatively changed, we may feel compelled to buy more of it this time around. Association is our brain's way of being lazy. We effectively say to ourselves, "Why bother objectively analyzing the risk / reward again when we know that buying the stock at around this price resulted in a good outcome before?" In part 3, I illustrate how association can lead to positive intuitive feelings about certain investments. However, we still need to balance these gut instincts with analysis.

Short Term Orientation

Another way to relieve stress is by getting some satisfaction quickly, or by avoiding investments that may be good over the long term but which have the possibility of losing money in the short term. In *Your*

Brain and Your Money, Jason Zweig argues that "an immediate gain gives you a jolt of dopamine that you cannot get from choosing a delayed reward."[32] Therefore, an investment where there is a perception of a fast payoff tends to demand a premium price. Researchers have also shown that anticipation of losses is much more painful than actually experiencing loss. Many of the best investors take advantage of others' short term orientation. They buy good long term investments when most seem overly concerned about short term events. They trim positions when they are extended ahead of highly anticipated positive news. Note that this doesn't mean that all short term trading strategies are flawed. Some good short term traders actually use this bias to their advantage. They anticipate how others will behave as certain events get closer.

Vulnerabilities Caused by Fluctuations in Mood

The final grouping of vulnerabilities involves fluctuations in mood. When we are happy, we are more inclined to take risks and be impulsive than when we are sad. Because investment gains can cause us to become even happier, we sometimes respond by becoming even more risk-seeking when we should be becoming less so.

Sadness and Depression

When we are depressed, we tend to want to change our lives. This can result in undervaluing what we own and overvaluing what we do not have. Dr. Jennifer Lerner of Harvard University speculates that this is why some people feel the need to go shopping when they are depressed.[33] While people generally hold on to losers to avoid feeling shame, sadness eventually catches up with them. The end result is what traders describe as capitulation. The depressed crowd reaches a point where their sadness has overcome their ability to think rationally, so they have to dump their investments no matter what the price. Many of these investors are too scarred from the losing investment to buy it back even when it becomes clear that fundamentals have improved. They may also not want to admit to themselves or others that they made a mistake by selling when they did. Finally, sadness often leads to excessive risk aversion.

Happiness

Happiness is the opposite of sadness specifically in that it can lead to poorly calculated risk-taking. Researchers have found that people who are happier are more impulsive. Since investment returns often positively impact people's moods, dangerous cycles can develop. As an investment starts to generate gains, people become happier. This change in mood can result in more risk-taking until the risk-taking is excessive and leads to losses. The losses eventually lead to sadness and capitulation. This is why the market continuously follows a cyclical pattern. The best investors try to not fall victim to significant changes in mood. They try to stay humble when others would be gloating. Similarly, the best investors remain upbeat when others would be feeling depressed.

Because the market moves in cycles from euphoria to despair, from low-volatility to nerve-racking, etc., a time may come when an investor's given style is not appropriate for the current environment. For example, value investors with long term investment horizons are frequently frustrated with the lack of buying opportunities when most in the market are optimistic and taking excessive risk. Similarly, short term traders, who thrive in the large day-to-day price movements of a highly volatile market, can become irritated with the lower short term profit potential that lower volatility offers.

Mood is contagious and leaders are very influential. According to Daniel Goleman, one of the foremost thought leaders on emotional intelligence, "In groups where there are power differences – in the classroom, at work, in organizations generally – it is the most powerful person who is the emotional sender, setting the emotional state for the rest of the group."[34] A leader whose mood swings wildly based on losses and gains in the firm's portfolio frequently amplifies the mood swings of employees. He can cause the entire firm to become even more depressed / risk-averse or happy / risk-seeking than otherwise may be the case.

There are many other variables that impact mood. Professors Trujillo and Knutson from Stanford University demonstrated that people are much more likely to make riskier and more impulsive decisions after simply viewing a picture of someone with a happy face. Subjects who were shown a fearful face, more often than not became more risk averse. The human tolerance for risk has even been proven to be correlated by such subtle things as the amount of sunlight in a given day, how well we sleep, how much alcohol we consume and the moods of the people around us.[35]

CHAPTER 4

Dealing with Vulnerabilities

"To others, being wrong is a source of shame. To me, recognizing my mistakes is a source of pride. Once we realize that imperfect understanding is the human condition, there's no shame in being wrong, only in failing to correct our mistakes." – George Soros, *Soros on Soros*

For a lucky few, self-awareness of their most common mistakes comes quickly. Most of us need a fair amount of time to reflect on the past. While I feel the process of writing down and reflecting on my blunders and triumphs has enabled me to understand myself much better, I still appreciate that there is much more to be done. Self-awareness is a very big first step. However, we only become set up for success after developing processes and strategies that safeguard us from repeatedly making the same mistakes. Being short in stature in the NBA is a major impediment. Nevertheless, there have been many relatively diminutive basketball players who have had successful professional careers. They are effective players because they are aware of their vulnerabilities. They focus on developing skills such as long-range shooting, ball-handling and passing, which do not necessarily require being big. While their personal heroes may have been 7-footers, great short players know that emulating them would be ridiculous. When a good small basketball player is tightly guarded by a much taller player, he knows that the best strategy is to not force up a shot that has a decent probability of getting blocked. Instead, he passes the ball or uses his superior speed to go around the defender. In the same way that a short basketball player cannot play like Shaquille O'Neal, we should not all try to have investment processes exactly like Warren Buffett. Just like the short basketball player, we each need to develop a strategy and process for improvement that fits our unique set of assets and liabilities. Therefore, dealing with vulnerability is highly personal. No book can provide a checklist that works for everyone. However, we can get ideas by looking at how some great investors and academics suggest managing specific issues. After a brief discussion regarding motivation, I give some examples of how the biases and mistakes covered in the previous chapter may be handled and how one can become more self-aware. There are many other methodologies one can use, and after reading this book you need to allow some time for introspection and trial and error to figure out what is best for you.

Understanding Motivation

Understanding motivation is a necessary initial step in self-awareness. When you ask most people why they invest, they simply say "to make money." However, you need to try to understand *why* you want to make money.[36] Is it so you can put food on the table and so your children will have a good education? If so, maybe you already have enough wealth and do not need to make risky investments at all. People who pursue risky investments that they do not need to make in order to achieve their life goals are generally more susceptible to stress once they have losses that put those goals at risk. They are also more prone to taking excess risk after losses. Are you driven because you like to be part of a team and to affiliate with others for a common goal? If so, maybe you need to reevaluate if you are in the correct role and with the right team? Are you motivated to make more money so that people will think more highly of you? If so, you may be susceptible to many of the biases discussed in the previous chapter that involve avoiding being "wrong." After all, if you are motivated by esteem, you may have a strong inner desire to be "right" most of the time. As we learned in the previous chapter, the desire of being "right" does not necessarily correlate with positive investment performance. Are you driven by the thrill of making money quickly? If so, you may need to modify your investment process to prevent becoming overly impulsive in making decisions or at least so that you can get out of mistakes quickly. Maybe power is what motivates you? If so, you need to better understand what drives the people you are trying to lead. You also should be especially aware of hindsight bias and how your mood can infect others. Whatever makes you tick, it is important to understand and accept it.

Dr. Richard Peterson states, "Rather than thinking in terms of making a lot of money, a much more productive frame is to focus specifically on what we'd like to achieve in life."[37] I followed this advice relatively well in my career up to a certain point. Being the eldest child of immigrants, I was originally motivated by the need to pay off student loans and to secure the basic needs for my family. After some early success, this inspiration became irrelevant; especially since my younger siblings were also well on their way to accumulating wealth of their own. My motivation then shifted towards achieving financial autonomy. I wanted to free myself from the bondages of employment. While the various jobs and mentors I had in my life had been crucial for my development, I aspired to be financially self-sufficient. I enjoyed the fulfillment that comes from hard work, but I desired to not *need* to work for others. After some reflection, I now realize that I became de-motivated after I had accumulated enough wealth to have achieved this goal. Without a new goal, I no longer understood why I was doing what I was doing. I started to feel more and more like a zombie following a daily routine. I have come to realize that the best long-lasting motivator for success is self-improvement based. Instead of focusing on how much money I make or whether I am wrong or right on a given investment, I try to put the focus on continuous learning and development. I try to welcome being "wrong." It helps me to become more self-aware. I better understand how to avoid similar mistakes in the future. The irony is that by welcoming being wrong, I actually make fewer slip-ups. I now feel relatively less susceptible to several human biases that involve the need to feel "right".

Some Ideas for How to Deal with Our Avoidance of Feeling Regret, Shame and Fear

The desire to avoid specific unwanted emotions can be a significant source of investing error. I have suggested some ways to cope based on the examples of a few great investors and the recommendations from psychologists. By no means is this meant to be a complete list.

Have a Sounding Board

According to Daniel Kahneman, "It is much easier to identify a minefield when you observe others wandering into it than when you are about to do so."[38] Other experienced investors are often much better at seeing you make a common investing mistake than you are. Moreover, when one is taking an unpopular stance, it can help psychologically to talk to a partner that has seen your analysis and agrees with your assessment. There are several successful investors who have had like-minded partners. Warren Buffett's partnership with Charlie Munger is probably the best-known example. Both Buffett and Munger strive to be independent thinkers. Instead of having a partner, many other investors find solace in conversing with a few other people who are thinking the same way as they are. This helps them to feel less lonely in their convictions, which can be the difference between staying in contrarian positions and abandoning them.

Stop-Losses

By selling after a certain percentage loss, traders can prevent holding on to their losers too long. However, there are some issues with stop-losses that make them inappropriate for every situation and every type of investor. For example, in environments where the overall market is very volatile, traders run the risk of covering many of their short positions after big up days in the market because of their stop-loss discipline. They may then be overexposed with their remaining long positions the following day if the market goes back down. Furthermore, many of the best investors actually buy on weakness. After all, unless there is a fundamental change, the investment they liked beforehand just got even more attractive. Instead of blindly exiting a position, because it lost them 10% for example, these value investors sell as soon as they recognize they are wrong.

Trim a Small Amount from Winners

Some fund managers like to trim a very small amount when they have gains even though they think the investments can potentially be worth much more. This may not be the most optimal money making strategy, but it placates their fear of regret. After trimming a small amount they feel like they are in a position to add the amount back in the event that the stock does go back down.

Avoid "Keeping Up with the Joneses"

Jason Zweig states, "A study of more than 7,000 people in over 300 towns and cities found that, on average, the more money the richest person in your community makes, and the greater the number of neighbors who earn more than you, the less satisfied you will probably feel with your life." Envy can cause an overemphasis on being "right." It can result in making the psychologically safe decision to just do what others do. People have taken different approaches to reducing the pressure to keep up with others. I have a friend that recently moved from New York City to be closer to his family in Philadelphia. By doing so, he went from being average in terms of net worth in his West Village neighborhood to being one of the more affluent in his new Pennsylvania community. Warren Buffett also shows that frugality can empower you to be less susceptible to the biases and negative emotions that arise when you compare yourself to others. For example, well before he became one of the world's richest men, many people in Omaha knew that he could afford a nicer house. Buffett demonstrates that sometimes by not playing the game of "keeping up with the Joneses," you can actually win at it.

Do Not Over-Commit

A simple rule many of the best investors use is to not make bets so large that they cannot afford being wrong. If you cannot afford being wrong, your self-defense mechanisms are even more likely to kick-in. For example, over-committing often makes traders more prone to overconfidence bias. It can also make investors susceptible to depression and to taking excess risk after losses to try to make the money back.

Visualize Failure and Its Causes

One of Paul Tudor Jones' rules for investing is to "always question yourself and your ability. Don't ever feel that you are very good. The second you do, you are dead."[39] Most analysts tend to focus on all the ways they will make money on an investment. While they may highlight risks, very few actually visualize failure. Before making an investment, I try to imagine it producing a loss. I then try to think about the possible reasons why I could be wrong. Sometimes, this exercise makes me think of risks I didn't think about before. It also makes me more prepared for and accepting of being wrong. Consequently, I have higher chances to sell a loser quickly and become less prone to overconfidence bias. Trading coach Brett Steenbarger preaches, "Self confidence is not expecting the best; it's knowing deep inside, that you can handle the worst."[40]

Imagine Creating a New Portfolio from Scratch

Peter Salovey, a psychologist at Yale University, advises to ask yourself, "If all my investments were liquidated now, and I had the cash in hand and the freedom to put it anywhere, what would my investment portfolio look like?" This exercise can be effective with the status quo bias. It can also help evince how biases such as realizing gains too early or holding losers too long, are impacting you. Several famous investors go one step further. For example, Stanley Druckenmiller from time to time liquidates most or all his positions so he and his analysts can mentally start building a portfolio again with a fresh, less biased mental state.

Be Regularly on the Lookout for Flaws in Your Thesis

George Soros keeps himself from becoming overconfident by actively trying to find the flaws in his thesis. While many investors view weaknesses of a thesis negatively, Soros thinks finding the weakness is his competitive advantage. By finding the flaw, he realizes what will make trends reverse before others do.

Be More Open Minded to Other Opinions

Travis Bradberry gives the following advice: "Approach everyone you encounter as though they have something valuable to teach you."[41] This is one of the best ways to remain flexible to change and to avoid overconfidence. Furthermore, some people seek out the objective advice of partners or other investors in order to help with not waiting too long to exit losing investments. It is generally more effective to ask others if they would buy an investment at current prices rather than asking if you should sell. If they present some good reasons for staying away, maybe you should exit. Finally, others' opinions can be invaluable when visualizing failure and discovering flaws in your investment thesis. Asking others to brainstorm how your idea could fail allows you to tap into different sets of experiences and to think of flaws you may not have thought of on your own. Like any good brainstorming session, you need to be careful with critiquing individual ideas too soon. The desire to be "right" often causes many people to argue when they should be listening. This tends to make others less willing to look into their experience set and think creatively.

Avoid Excess Reputational Risk

Jesse Livermore, the great speculator from the early 20th century, rarely gave any tips. He probably knew that doing so would make it more difficult for him to change his mind. Being public about investment decisions can make some people overly focused on being "right" and can cause overconfidence. When your reputation is on the line, risk / reward decisions are further complicated by an additional non-monetary risk that can cloud optimal decision-making.

Expand the Timeframe of Stock Charts

A common mistake is to overly fixate or anchor on short term price movements. You believe a security is worth much more than the current price. Yet, you may hesitate to purchase, because you missed a recent large move. It is very rare to invest right at the bottom. One way to deal with the mental trap of anchoring is to expand the timeframe of the stock charts. For example, if you see that the stock is down 70% over the last three years even after the recent 8% move that you just missed, it may make you feel much better about at least buying some today.

Avoid Auctions

Warren Buffett and Charlie Munger avoid participating in auctions for new acquisitions. Oaktree's Howard Marks also describes how his firm tries to only negotiate with desperate sellers.[42] By avoiding auctions, you can sidestep the biases that come from feeling like you already have something that you don't.

Some Ideas for How to Deal with Stress and Mental Overload

Our brains have a finite capacity to digest and process information. There are several ways to successfully manage this limitation. Some of the most common methodologies are described below.

Preparedness

Imagine having to engage in a debate on an unfamiliar topic with only 10 minutes to prepare. You will be much more stressed than if you had a lot time to read everything available related to the topic. Being prepared generally reduces fear and stress. Preparedness comes from learning as much as possible about a given topic, and from visualizing how your investment will do and how you will feel in a range of scenarios. There were several times in my career when I felt I understood a given company and its industry just as well as or better than any other financial analyst. The preparedness allowed me to more easily separate noise from fundamental changes that impacted my thesis. I took advantage of when others were surprised and I was not. While random events still surprised me from time to time, I knew that if I was surprised, most others would be surprised too. I was confident in my ability to more quickly understand implications for both the given investment and for other related companies. Bruce Kovner, founder of The Caxton Group, describes one of his main competitive advantages as his ability to visualize different scenarios. He said, "I have the ability to imagine configurations of the world different from today and really believe it can happen. I can imagine that soybean prices can double or that the dollar can fall to 100 yen."[43] As described earlier, the drawback of the sunk cost of time invested in getting prepared is that it can lead to overconfidence. There is tremendous value in being better prepared, but we need to use self-awareness and some techniques – such as those described in this chapter – to safeguard us from becoming overconfident.

Rely on Your Own Work

After being asked what advice he would give to novice traders, Michael Marcus, a famous trader formerly at Commodities Corporation, said "If it comes down to 'I am in this trade because Bruce is in it,' then you are not going to have the courage to stick with it. So you might as well not be in it in the first place."[44] As discussed previously, the best way to reduce stress and fear is by having as much control as possible. Relying on someone else's work simply does not put you in control. There is nothing wrong with listening or reading about the ideas of others, but in the end, you need to do your own analysis and make decisions that fit an investing style based on your own personal set of strengths, weakness, motivations and personality characteristics. Relying on your own work also helps with dealing with the fear of regret. For example, one of my friends regularly tells me about his favorite stock ideas. Whenever his recommended stocks are significantly outperforming, I inevitably get a call from him and he usually says the same thing: "You need to buy these stocks. They are going much higher." In the past, I would often buy small amounts of the recommended stocks. After keeping a journal and tracking these types of decisions, I now realize that I mainly bought his recommendations because I feared feeling regret. If the stocks continued to go up, I did not want to continue to miss out on the gains. I feared admitting to him that I did not follow his advice. While my friend is a good investor, I also discovered that following his recommendations blindly was not making me money. His style was different from mine and I inevitably got scared out of holding investments (which I did not fully understand) at the most inopportune times.

Maintain a Simple Process

In *The Four Filters Invention of Warren Buffett & Charlie Munger,* Bud Labitan illustrates that the famous duo conduct a relatively simple process when evaluating an investment. They first ask themselves if they understand the business. If yes, they then ask themselves if the company has a long term competitive advantage. If so, they then ask themselves how they feel about the management's honesty and abilities. If the investment idea makes it through that filter, they make sure they are getting a reasonable price for the investment.[45] Buffett and Munger are aware of their own tendencies to become overconfident as more of their time is invested researching an idea. They also realize that sometimes too much information can cloud judgment. Buffett and Munger deal with these biases by having a relatively simple process. They do not make detailed financial forecasts. Unlike many private equity firms with whom they compete, they also do not use an army of consultants to conduct due diligence.

Limit the Number of Positions and Spend Time Prioritizing the To-Do List

Increased portfolio concentration increases risk. However, the more positions one has, the more trading decisions are needed and the more news needs to be digested. Most portfolio managers say that the top few winners in any given year disproportionally impact performance. Charlie Munger once said, "If you took our top fifteen decisions out, we'd have a pretty average record."[46] It is clear that significant stress can be reduced if one mainly spends time working on the right investments. While most firms have set up processes for analyzing investments, they generally spend little time on prioritization of the to-do list. Working long hours to analyze many potential ideas can be a waste of time, if not enough thought is put into what one should be working on. Later in the book, I discuss how intuition from the most experienced in an organization should be harnessed to prioritize a firm's idea pipeline.

Adjust Stop Orders Instead of Overtrading

Recall that when you are stressed, doing *something* feels better than doing nothing. In *Stop Orders*, the financial writer and trader, Tony Loton argues that periodically adjusting stop orders can be a remedy for overtrading. He states, "Adjusting a stop order gives me something to do in the market without costing me a penny."[47] For example, if a stock you are invested in rises from $40 to $60, don't sell "too soon" at this price if you think that the correct valuation is much higher. Instead, adjust your stop order to sell at $54 to take you out at profit if the trend reverses, while at the same time allowing for an even higher profit if the trend continues (just like you expect it to).

Do Not Multitask

According to David Brooks, "A person who is interrupted while performing a task takes 50% more time to complete it and makes 50% more errors. The brain doesn't multitask well. It needs to get into a coherent flow, with one [neural] network of firings leading coherently to the next."[48]Unlike virtually every other hedge fund, Greenlight Capital does not give their analysts smartphones. During investment conferences, most analysts seem to be more focused on their blackberries than the corporate management teams making the presentations. I noticed that Greenlight's analysts always paid much more attention to what was being said in meetings. Many analysts at Greenlight also do not have real-time quotes on their Bloomberg screens. Greenlight is not a firm that trades very actively; therefore, the firm knows that looking at a computer screen with hundreds of moving numbers is an unnecessary distraction for most of its employees. One longer term oriented investor I talked to tries to only check his email on three given set periods in a day. He also forces himself to look at his Bloomberg screen and make trading decisions only in the morning and just before the market closes. He generally feels less stressed and more focused. He is in control of his day as opposed to allowing the market to be in command of him. As related earlier, feeling like you are in control makes you less susceptible to fear. He is also less susceptible to errors that result from too much noise / information. This takes tremendous discipline and may not be appropriate for shorter term traders.

Checklists

Charlie Munger believes that "checklists are almost always helpful."[49] Before making any serious investment decision, some people may benefit by quickly going through the above list of common mistakes and asking themselves if they think they may be falling for one of the traps. This is another way to become more self-aware of vulnerabilities without actually having to financially suffer from making the errors.

Breathing

It sounds simple, but deep breathing has been shown to improve decision-making. Because the other parts of the brain are considered more vital, the prefrontal cortex and other rational brain centers are last in line for receiving oxygen, especially when we are stressed. Therefore, taking a deep breath before making a decision can be helpful in boosting rational processing power and focus. The time it takes to take a deep breath can also simply be a buffer useful from becoming too impulsive.

Snacking

Maybe even more obvious than breathing is making sure that the brain has enough glucose to operate effectively. Daniel Kahneman states, "The nervous system consumes more glucose than most other parts of the body, and effortful mental activity appears to be especially expensive in the currency of glucose." In his book, *Thinking, Fast and Slow*, Kahneman describes a number of research studies that demonstrate how people who are given even a small amount of sugar do much better at tasks that involve the rational centers of the brain. Other studies show that people are inclined to make their worst analytical decisions immediately before meals. This is when glucose levels are most depleted.[50]

Other Ways to Relax

Because high stress can reduce focus and negatively impact decision-making, we should find ways to relax as best we can. David Einhorn regularly takes naps on a couch in his office. Pimco's Bill Gross does yoga almost every morning. Carl Icahn reportedly takes a bath every evening.[51] Sir John Templeton was very religious and supposedly started many meetings with a prayer. I find taking frequent breaks from sitting at my desk and walking around is helpful. There are many great investors who make exercise a part of their daily routine. Exercise has been shown to produce growth hormones that relieve stress. Finally, many investors find meditation useful as well.

Some Ideas for How to Deal with Changes in Mood

Mood swings impact our level of risk aversion and, because they are contagious, influence a market's cyclicality. Without a process for either managing or understanding the fluctuations in our mood, we risk falling victim to the boom-bust cycles of the market. Some approaches are outlined below.

Take Inventory of Emotional State Before Making Big Decisions

It can be useful to write down in a journal what type of mood you are in. The better we can understand our feelings, the better we will be able to control and recognize how they impact our decision-making. I read about one trader who does this every morning. He believes it helps him to regulate his appetite for risk. For example, when he notes that he is in a very happy mood, he tries to be even more cautious than normal. On very happy days, he forces himself to count to ten before conducting any trade.

Focus on Self-Improvement Instead of Outcomes

We need to do our best to break the dangerous cycle of investment returns impacting our mood. The best way to do this is by not focusing on outcomes, but on the process you used to make decisions. Most of us also have a tendency to anchor off our peak net worth or the high point of the portfolio in the current year. As Dr. Richard Peterson says, fixating on numbers like these "will create an itch, one that you will seek to scratch at great cost to your mental health and net worth."[52] Anchoring off these numbers either makes us sad and excessively risk averse or leads us to take excess risk to get back "even" with the high point. Either reaction leads to suboptimal decision-making over the long term.

Actively Regulate Mood

Leaders of most firms exacerbate mood fluctuations. I once worked for someone who did not like to see people in the office joke around and laugh when the firm's portfolio was having a bad day. Since we know that bad decisions can result from being too happy or too sad, a better approach is to try to create an environment that counteracts mood swings. I read about one portfolio manager that threw a firm party when the firm hit a rough patch. Changing art in the office has also been shown to have an impact on mood. Putting up photographs of the Great Depression after the firm's performance has been stellar can slightly dampen the mood so that people do not become too risk-seeking. The better leaders are somber when most in the firm are enthusiastic and are more cheerful when weak performance leads to organizational melancholy.

CHAPTER 5

Matching Personality to Investment Style

"As long as you stick to your own style, you get the good and bad of your own approach. When you try to incorporate someone else's style, you often wind up with the worst of both styles." – Michael Marcus, *Market Wizards*

As described in the prior chapters, fluctuations of mood cause changes in tolerance of risk. Since we tend to be happier as our portfolio does better, we become more impulsive and risk-seeking in bull markets and more cautious and risk-averse in bear markets. This tendency, combined with our inclination to herd and the fact that mood is highly contagious, is why the market constantly fluctuates between booms and busts. According to Howard Marks, "The mood swings of the securities markets resemble the movement of a pendulum. Although the midpoint of its arc describes the location of the pendulum on average, it actually spends very little of its time there. Instead, it is almost always swinging toward or away from the extremes of its arc."[53] There are two general investing styles which take advantage of the swinging pendulum. Value investing involves trying to make money by guessing that the pendulum is near the end of its swing, all the way to the left or all the way to the right, and that it should eventually swing the other way. Growth or Momentum investing involves betting that the pendulum will continue in its current direction, left to right (let's call it "bullish") or right to left (let's call it "bearish"). Success in each of these styles generally requires distinct personality traits and strengths. Within each of these approaches, an investment horizon can be either long term or short term. Investment horizon largely depends on what an individual finds most interesting about investing.

Figure 1: The Investment Pendulum

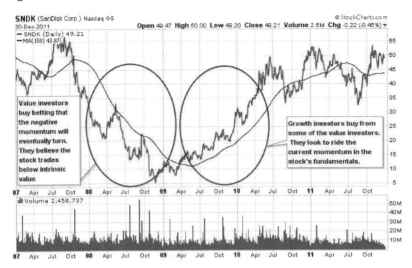

Value investors include people like Benjamin Graham, Seth Klarman and Howard Marks. They usually have no view with respect to timing. While they think that there is a large discrepancy between current valuation and the intrinsic valuation (with this discrepancy represented by the metaphorical pendulum's position to the "bearish" left or "bullish" right of the mid-point of the pendulum's swing), they do not necessarily know when the pendulum will change its direction. They are prepared to lose money and add to their investments if the current trend continues. Many of these investors take comfort in a margin of safety that theoretically limits how far the pendulum will go. For example, Benjamin Graham would highlight net working capital less debt on a company's balance sheet as a proxy for liquidation value. It is very rare to be able to invest precisely at an inflection point; therefore, investors who take a stand against the tide should *expect* to initially lose money. Researchers have demonstrated that pain has a diminishing impact with respect to losses. For example, we feel more pain on the first $10,000 we lose on an investment than the next $10,000 loss. Consequently, adopting an investing style where one is likely to initially lose money on most new

66

positions is not for everyone. People who thrive in this style are those that are relatively less susceptible towards the impulse to herd and those that are generally more patient for obtaining rewards. Value investors also tend to be more cautious and more thorough in their analysis than others. And it is helpful to be less emotionally sensitive so that losses do not necessarily impact future decisions. Finally, successful investors in this group generally avoid over-committing. They visualize how they will feel if the current momentum continues and they lose money. They only invest an amount so that initial losses are bearable and so that they can have enough in reserve to add to positions as they fall in value.

Growth or Momentum investors include people such as T. Rowe Price, Jesse Livermore, George Soros and Ed Seykota. Investors who bet with the momentum are more likely to make money initially, but can suffer huge losses when the momentum inevitably shifts. The key to success with this style is to anticipate when a trend is starting to go the wrong way. Successful investors in this group are less susceptible to waiting too long to sell losers and do not become overconfident. They are also less inclined to take on more risk after losses by adding to positions on weakness. Instead, many in this group employ stop-losses and will frequently add to their winners at higher prices. They are less prone to status quo bias and treat every day as a new day that could have a completely new portfolio. While their win / loss ratios may be impressive, they do not focus on it and instead try to keep themselves from becoming overconfident. They know that even just one big loser can ruin returns. Furthermore, growth or momentum investors are generally less susceptible to the anchoring bias. Jesse Livermore once said, "Don't worry about catching the tops or bottoms. It's fools play."[54] Unlike value investors, growth investors need not be very cautious with their initial investment, but need to be more cautious after the investment is made. The best are constantly on the lookout for fundamental news that proves them wrong. Growth investors are generally less risk-averse than value investors. They are also usually more extroverted.

In reality, most investors take a hybrid approach. For example, John Paulson bet against the pendulum's momentum by shorting the housing market and initially lost money. However, he significantly increased his bets in 2007 after it became obvious to him that the momentum had shifted. Stanley Druckenmiller and George Soros had an initial position against the British Pound for some time in 1992. They knew that an inflection point was coming, but did not know when. When it finally became obvious to them that Sterling would be devalued, they increased their position significantly and are now revered / reviled for "breaking the Bank of England."[55] Paul Tudor Jones is another successful investor that employs a hybrid approach. While he is not a traditional value investor who tries to understand intrinsic value, he often takes positions against the momentum of the pendulum. In *Market Wizards*, Jones evinced high self-awareness when he said, "I have very strong views of the long-run directions of all markets. I also have a very short term horizon for pain."[56] His strength is to know when the pendulum has swung too far and he has an intuitive feel for the timing of inflections. For example, he is probably most famous for calling the market crash in October 1987 and returning 62% for his investors that month. However, Jones knows that he is not like Seth Klarman and other more typical value investors who "fight the pendulum's momentum." He knows he will lose his emotional equilibrium if he experiences large losses or has to wait too long for gains. Therefore, like growth investors, he rarely ever adds to his losing positions and will often add to his winning investments at higher prices as it becomes even more evident that the momentum has shifted. He limits his mistakes through stop-losses and liquidates his position if the reversal of momentum does not occur in the timeframe he was originally looking for.

The key factor that drives the holding period in either investing approach is motivation. Because most value investors have almost no view as to when their bets will start to pay off, most have longer term investment horizons. Some value investors, like Warren Buffett and Charlie Munger, plan to hold their investments for their entire lives. While Buffett and Munger like to buy below intrinsic value, they also look for companies that can predictably grow intrinsic value significantly over time. These companies usually have high sustainable competitive advantages and high returns on capital. Nevertheless, not all investors that bet against momentum are long term investors. Paul Tudor Jones is an example of someone that often fights a current trend, but who can also have a relatively short holding period. Jones seems to enjoy investing because he likes predicting investor psychology. Seth Klarman enjoys investing, because he likes finding bargains as defined by market valuations that are significantly below intrinsic valuations. Buffett enjoys learning about businesses' long term competitive advantages. Their respective motivations explain why Jones is a short term trader, why Klarman is a long term investor and why Buffett looks to hold his investments forever. Unlike value investing, growth investing tends to have many short term traders. Status quo bias can be particularly dangerous. Growth investors have to be constantly paranoid about the reversal of momentum. Consequently, most growth investors frequently adjust their portfolios to reflect their latest thoughts regarding the trends they are involved in. That being said, there are some growth investors, who hold their positions for a very long time. Steve Mandel at Lone Pine Capital is an example of a growth investor that has held many positions for several years. Mandel seems to like investing, because he relishes developing views regarding long term secular growth trends. Other money managers, like Stanley Druckenmiller, enjoy developing a differentiated view versus consensus over the short or medium term. They also enjoy predicting investor psychology. Again motivation explains why Mandel has a longer investment horizon than most other growth investors.

Many investors are effective using both investment styles. If a value investor "fights the pendulum" on an investment and the momentum eventually shifts, he is likely to have an unrealized gain. If this value investor does not fall for the trap of selling his winner too early and the pendulum's momentum continues, he now needs to be more like the successful investors in the second group and be constantly on the lookout for when the trend may reverse. Problems often arise when people get confused with what style they should be using. For example, in early 1996, Julian Robertson, founder of Tiger Management, made a contrarian investment in US Airways. By the summer of 1998, the investment was up over 400% and worth $1.5 billion. The momentum on US Airways' stock had clearly shifted yet Robertson still dealt with it in a "fighting the pendulum" frame of mind. In early 1999, US Airways reported weak quarterly results and the stock declined 29% in three weeks. Instead of recognizing a shift in momentum and reducing his position, Robertson wrote to his investors that he expected the stock to triple. The stock continued to drift lower throughout 1999 despite the overall bull market.[57]

In the US Airways example above, Julian Robertson ended up applying the incorrect investment approach after the stock did very well. Another common mistake is to mismatch investing style with the thesis at the time of the investment. For example, in 2006 all the US homebuilding stocks had more than a decade of strong gains. The homebuilders had been benefiting from several trends such as mortgage rates that had been declining for some time and sharp increases in home prices across the country. The US homebuilders were clearly stocks that were experiencing significant positive momentum. Nevertheless, most of the analysts who recommended the securities primarily highlighted their relatively low price-to-earnings ratios. They used a value investing approach when they should have used a growth investing approach. Value investors commonly justify their investments using valuation support. However, valuation should only be a secondary factor for companies and industries that have been benefiting from favorable long term trends. Instead, investors that bet on companies, which have been significantly benefiting from trends, should primarily highlight their differentiation with respect to consensus earnings expectations or how they think factors that have been in the company's favor may even get better. Since many investors in the homebuilders used the incorrect approach, they did not immediately exit their investments when it started to become clear that the housing market was weakening. They did not realize that the pendulum's movement had shifted. Instead, some of them added to their losing investments. They continued to cling to the fact that earnings multiples were extremely low. By 2010, the homebuilding stocks were down significantly from their peaks, and because earnings had declined they no longer had very low price-to-earnings ratios. In most cases, earnings were actually negative.

In addition to being introspective with respect to your motivations and the common mental traps you are most susceptible to, it is necessary to consider other aspects of your personality before developing your own investment style. Unlike aspects of emotional intelligence such as social awareness, which can significantly improve with effort, personality traits are relatively unchanging after the teenage years. There are many theories that describe personality, but the most influential is the "Big Five" model. The variables of personality considered in this model are extraversion, agreeableness, conscientiousness, emotional sensitivity and openness. Extraversion involves how chatty, energetic and emphatic one tends to be. Agreeableness is the inclination to be kind and sympathetic. Conscientiousness refers to the tendency to be thorough and organized. Emotionality is the inclination to be moody and stressed. Openness refers to the predisposition to be imaginative and to have broad interests. You need to conduct some self-reflection to understand your personality across these dimensions.

Extroverts have a tendency to be more risk-seeking than introverts. A drawback is that extroverts are usually more susceptible to herding. Agreeable people are nice to be around so they may have an advantage in their ability to gather information. However, self-interested people may be more comfortable in highly competitive environments. Conscientious investors generally conduct more thorough analysis. Those who are impulsive may have difficulty with the value investing approach that is likely to initially lose money. People who have low emotionality may be better at "fighting the pendulum's momentum" and sustaining losses, while those who are more emotionally sensitive may need to routinely employ stop-losses to maintain their psychological equilibrium. Open people appreciate the viewpoint of others and value individualism. This makes them less susceptible to overconfidence, status quo bias and to herding. However, those who are less open may do better in markets that follow an established trend for long periods of time.

As described earlier, Paul Tudor Jones recognizes his emotionality. He knows that large losses or waiting too long to have a gain on a position can negatively impact his decision-making. Consequently, Jones developed a style which takes this aspect of his personality into account. He places small initial bets. Jones then stops himself out when investments go against him or if they do not work after a certain period of time. If his trades do work, he takes this as confirmation of his hypothesis and adds to the positions at higher prices. He also realizes he needs to safeguard his emotional sensitivity. He told Jack Schwager, "I know that to be successful, I have to be frightened. My biggest hits have always come after I have had a great period and I started to think that I knew something."[58] Similar to Jones, George Soros knows that he can be impulsive. His investing style offsets the drawbacks of impulsiveness with a relentless drive to find the flaws in his theories. In *Open Society*, Soros states, "I derived actual pleasure from discovering a mistake."[59] He often sells or even reverses his position after realizing the error in his hypothesis. In *Buffett: The Making of an American Capitalist*, author Roger Lowenstein describes Warren Buffett as someone who is somewhat introverted with high conscientiousness and relatively low emotionality. Buffett's children talk about how they rarely saw their father cry, for example. Buffett's investing style, which is very long term in nature, takes advantage of these personality traits. He employs his conscientiousness by only investing in companies that he comprehensively understands and that have strong sustainable competitive advantages. For example, he avoids most technology companies because he cannot envision how they will be in 10+ years, given technological obsolescence risks. Unrealized losses do not seem to have much, if any, emotional impact on Buffett. Thus, he is capable of adding to his positions on weakness when others may be capitulating.

Another important trait is one's tolerance for ambiguity. People derive confidence with different levels of uncertainty. For example, Secretary of State Colin Powell once remarked that if he was more than 70% confident, he probably wasted too much time and resources gathering information.[60] My wife, on the other hand, can spend *half an hour* going over a restaurant menu and still not be 70% confident in her final decision. Unlike the Big Five personality traits, which are relatively unchanging, one's tolerance for uncertainty seems to fluctuate somewhat with factors, such as mood, that impact one's risk aversion. When we are doing well with our portfolios, we tend to be happier, which causes us to have a higher tolerance for ambiguity when making decisions.

The psychologist Gary Klein has identified five sources of uncertainty. They are missing information, unreliable information, conflicting information, noisy information and confusing information.[61] Different investing styles deal with these sources of uncertainty differently. Most people take an incremental approach. They initially take a small position or none at all, and as uncertainty declines they add to their positions. The issue with this common technique is that it is common. The overall market does the same thing so you wind up buying at higher prices as the uncertainty is reduced. Often, the uncertainty is what is creating the opportunity for outsized returns. The best investors have developed means to gain conviction while others are still less certain. Warren Buffett frequently takes advantage of noisy and confusing uncertainty about the short term. Since he has a very long time horizon, he does not necessarily care about any uncertainty regarding the information concerning a company's immediate financial results. Other investors spend a lot of time and money doing survey work to find information that the market considers missing. For example, they may call or visit a bunch of video game and consumer electronic stores to develop a view towards how Activision Blizzard's latest video game is selling. They do this before Activision Blizzard reports its earnings or before brokerage analysts do similar analysis. Peter Lynch, formerly at Fidelity, advises individual investors to reduce uncertainty by investing in trends and products they are familiar with. For example, he would tell someone that plays video games frequently that she is likely to have an informational edge with Activision Blizzard's stock if she and her friends have a strong view regarding the company's latest product. Some investors frequently hire lawyers or consultants to help them better trust and interpret information. Value investors like Seth Klarman from The Baupost Group take comfort in a company's balance sheet or intrinsic value and simply base decisions on risk and reward. They say to themselves something like "I have no idea where the economy is headed, but if it stays bad, the worst I lose is x since that is the company's liquidation value. If the uncertainty about the economy goes away, I think the company could be worth y with a relatively high probability." If y is much greater than x, they make an investment and as the stock approaches x, they simply buy more. Another approach is to use technical analysis to get comfortable with uncertainty. For example, if there is a strong support level slightly lower, a trader may be more willing to make an investment with a certain amount of missing information. If the support level is very far away, it may be prudent to be less willing to make the same investment and wait for more clarity.

A final consideration before developing an investing approach is to understand what risk means to you in the current moment. For some, risk means holding on to a job. For others it means losing everything. Risk can also be perceived as underperformance in a given time period. As I related earlier in the book, one of my longtime motivations was to be free from *needing* to work for someone else. While I enjoy investing simply for my personal account, I am open to working at another firm someday. However, I do not want to feel like I *need* to. Thus, for me risk means losing the financial independence I value so much. After I quit my last job, I determined a minimum net worth I would need to maintain. Therefore, I have tailored my investing approach and my lifestyle so that I have almost no chance to go below this minimum threshold. As my portfolio appreciates and hopefully gets further from this threshold, I will become more willing to take risk. Similarly, if my wife and I have triplets and my future expenditures unexpectedly rise, I may need to raise this minimum net worth threshold and take less risk. I have learned that it is vital to be introspective with respect to what risk means to me. Since its meaning can be quite dynamic, it is something

I regularly reflect on in my journal. It impacts the sizing of my positions, my tolerance for uncertainty and how much exposure I am willing to take on the overall market's direction.

In the end there is no set rule for what style fits with each personality. Extroverts with high emotionality may be better off betting with the trend. However, Paul Tudor Jones has high emotionality and frequently bets against the current momentum of the pendulum. He uses stop-losses to limit the psychological pain inflicted by loss. We each need to conduct some experimentation and reflection to determine what style works best for us. Brett Steenbarger says, "Most traders who have not found their niche have never *played* with the markets. They haven't tried to trade different styles, different instruments, and different time frames... Elite performers never stop playing. Artists sketch; athletes play in scrimmages; actors improvise. Play is a means of self-discovery."[62] It is very difficult to develop a style that fits your unique set of attributes best by just imitating others. What you find most interesting about investing should help you to define your investment horizon. Shorter term traders are generally most interested in understanding and predicting investor psychology. They also enjoy developing differentiated views regarding short and medium term fundamentals. Longer term investors enjoy understanding long term secular growth trends or a company's sustainable competitive advantages, or they just like to find bargains trading well below intrinsic value. Once an investment approach is developed that fits you and what you like most about investing, it is important that recruiting involves screening for candidates that have personalities and motivations that also appropriately match the desired approach. For example, an analyst who is very emotionally sensitive, impulsive and who primarily enjoys predicting investor psychology will most probably not be a good fit working for Seth Klarman at Baupost.

I personally try to utilize both styles and I have developed a relatively strict set of rules that I apply with each approach:

- **My rules for investments that require a growth investing approach:** When I invest in companies that have been beating Wall Street's expectations and which clearly have momentum in their favor, I make it a rule to have a stop-loss. I also try to stay disciplined to not "dollar cost average" down with this type of investment. Instead, I may add as the position becomes a winner and I become more confident in my thesis. I am constantly on the lookout for a change in momentum. For example, if the company has been beating consensus estimates for several quarters in a row and then misses estimates, I get out. The thesis for investing in these types of securities should be based on some type of differentiation with consensus expectations either with respect to earnings or with respect to sustainability of growth. I think valuation is important, but it should not be the primary reason for investing in names that fall into this category.

- **My rules for investments that require a value investing approach:** I initially ask myself why I want to bet against the current momentum. Do I think the security is trading at a significant discount to its intrinsic value? Or do I have a view of a timeframe for when the momentum will shift? Or both? If the primary reason I am involved in the investment is because I believe it is significantly undervalued, I do not use stop-losses. Instead, I determine a very low valuation and add to the position as it approaches this "no-brainer" price. If I find the idea appealing mainly because I have certain catalysts in mind that will shift the direction of the pendulum, I sell if nothing happens in the timeframe I expect. I also will employ a stop-loss in this situation, but am willing to take more pain than if it was a company already benefiting from positive trends in its business fundamentals and valuation.

The key is making sure I apply the correct set of rules with the appropriate investments. As we saw with the example of the homebuilder stocks, incorrectly doing so can be very dangerous. Many great investors stick predominately with just one approach to limit confusion, but that also limits the universe of possible investments one can make. Before an investment is made, I make sure to note what methodology I am using with each security. Furthermore, to avoid making the same mistake Julian Robertson did with US Airways, I also find it useful to quickly reevaluate if I am using the correct approach with each investment every week. I use a couple of rules of thumb to help. First, if the company has been recently performing well, beating consensus expectations or is highly expected to beat expectations, it is most probably a company that requires a growth investing approach. Second, if the stock price is above its 150 day moving average and the moving average is sloping upward, it is also more likely to require a growth investing mindset. Conversely, if the company has been missing Wall Street's expectations or is expected to miss expectations going forward, the momentum is most probably for the stock price to go lower. The same is likely true if the stock is currently below its 150 day moving average and the moving average is trending downward. I use the 150 day moving average, but some may prefer the 100 day or the 200 day moving averages. They are all just proxies for how the stock has been performing. There are certainly exceptions to these rules, especially with respect to the second rule regarding the stock's relation to its 150 day moving average. Sometimes it is not very clear which category a specific stock should fall into. For example, what do you do with a company that has been consistently missing Wall Street's expectations and whose stock is below its moving averages, but you highly expect the company to be exactly in-line with expectations for the next couple of quarters? Often this type of situation can indicate an inflection point, where the stock starts to have positive momentum, even though the company is not yet beating consensus expectations. These rules of thumb are not perfect. However, I have found that when it is too difficult to determine which category a security should be in, time is usually better spent on other possible investments that are less difficult.

After leaving the hedge fund industry, Apple's stock (AAPL) was one of the first securities I bought with my personal money. The company had been doing extremely well for several years. The stock was well above its upward sloping 150 day moving average. Therefore, I viewed it as requiring a growth investing approach even though its price-to-earnings ratio was relatively low. I sold AAPL in July 2012 after the company missed quarterly expectations. That was the first significant miss for Apple in a very long time. Consequently, I viewed it as a negative change in momentum. Most financial analysts following Apple thought the quarter was a short term hiccup. This may be the case and I may end up buying AAPL back one day at a higher price if the company regains its upward trend. However, I find speculating on a growth stock regaining its momentum can be very dangerous. I would only bet on a change in momentum with AAPL if it had a more severe and prolonged downward trend. Only then would I be comfortable in taking a value investing approach.

CHAPTER 6

Developing Self-Awareness

"I suggest getting to know your feelings, by experiencing them, expressing them, letting them pass through and finding out they are pretty much all good ones." – Ed Seykota[63]

Hopefully, by now you understand why self-awareness in investing is so important. There is no one personality type that correlates to a better investor. What matters most is to know how to safeguard yourself from the specific mistakes you are most prone to make and to develop an investing strategy that best fits with your individual personality traits and motivations. However, for most, becoming more self-aware is not easy. Getting to know yourself requires daily effort. It is a continuous process with no clear endpoint. In Chapter 3, I laid out the most common biases and mistakes investors make. You may have recognized your own propensity for some of these vulnerabilities just from reading about them. That is a good start. Nevertheless, in order to be better aware of your weaknesses and to understand how you may best deal with them, it is essential to regularly analyze your decision-making process. Furthermore, you need to better understand your specific personality traits and motivations to ensure that your investing style is optimized for who you are. In this chapter, I provide some strategies to help advance self-awareness. They are suggestions from psychologists that specialize in emotional intelligence and from trading coaches. Some of these strategies for self-reflection are also derived from the daily and weekly routines of the world's historically best investors. The list below is not complete. You may think of another strategy that works best for you. What is vital is that self-analysis becomes a daily routine in whatever way you think is best. Most investors concede that reading the newspaper every morning is a necessary task. A similar daily emphasis on introspection is at least as important.

Confront Discomfort

Most of us are programmed to avoid negative feelings. We would much rather think about our good decisions instead of our bad ones. For example, many will not want to admit to themselves that they hold on to their losers too long because they fear feeling shame. Travis Bradberry states, "The biggest obstacle to increasing your self-awareness is the tendency to avoid the discomfort that comes from seeing yourself as you really are."[64]   Therefore, introspection needs to start with a willingness to understand the parts of yourself that you may not be proud of. While self-examination may temporarily bruise your ego, you will be much better off in the long-run.

Write in a Journal

Almost every psychologist and trading coach recommends keeping a journal. This is because there have been over 200 research projects that demonstrate how writing is beneficial. James Pennebaker of the University of Texas is the academic most associated with this field of research. He states, "an increasing number of studies indicate that having people write about emotional upheavals can result in healthy improvements in social, psychological, behavioral, and biological functioning."[65] Writing enables us to analyze our feelings. When we write about our emotions and how they impacted our decisions, we effectively create a bridge between our rational left brain and our more emotional and creative right brain. There are many approaches to keeping a journal. I write a short daily entry where I mainly focus on my mistakes and what I did well. I try to focus on my emotional state when prior decisions were made. Other investors and trading coaches recommend placing much more attention on what you are currently feeling. For example, Brett Steenbarger says, "When you experience a horrific trading day, give it voice. Talk it through and sear its lessons in your mind. If you're in touch with how badly your trading mistakes make you feel, you're less likely to repeat your errors. There can be gain in embracing pain"[66] Many studies from James Pennebaker and other researchers have demonstrated that writing not only brings about increased self-awareness, but it also is therapeutic. Therefore, in addition to being a good tool for self-examination, writing helps to maintain emotional equilibrium and to manage stress.

Examine Whether You Are Sticking to Your Investment Principles

Similar to the journal writing described above, another useful exercise from time to time is to make a list of the principles that fit with the investing strategy you have espoused. For example, Warren Buffett's list would probably include items such as "only invest in companies I understand," "only invest in companies with sustainable competitive advantages," and "only invest with competent management teams that I trust." Some traders even find it helpful to document their principles in books, articles, blogs, etc. for public consumption. After you have reviewed your most important investing principles, then make another list of decisions you have recently made that violated one of these core investing values. Most investors make many decisions every day and it is common for people to take action contrary to their core beliefs from time to time. However, unless you take the time to reflect on your core beliefs, and why certain decisions were made, you risk being an investor that has a good sales pitch but mediocre returns. The lack of discipline to your stated strategy inevitably will increase. Instead of being in control, you will allow others and the market to control you.

Monitor Physical Changes

Most emotions impact our bodies in some way. Various muscles tighten; the heart rate increases; the skin perspires; the mouth dries up, etc. It's often easier to recognize physical changes than the emotions themselves. Therefore, it can be helpful to try to monitor how certain emotions impact you physically. For example, George Soros learned to connect acute pain in his back with his intuition for sensing danger. He would not understand his gut feelings and they may have been contradictory to his analysis, but he learned to trust them. He would often reverse his positions when the pain set in. Another example is that I know that when the muscles in my scalp tighten up that I am overly stressed. I often sense those muscles tightening before I recognize my high stress level. This connection helps me to try to be proactive in avoiding some of the pitfalls associated with stress. When you watch a movie and feel a distinct emotion, try to connect the feeling with your physical changes. The next time you sense those same bodily changes, you are probably also feeling that same specific emotion.

Seek Feedback

We are living in an increasingly narcissistic society. According to psychologist Jean Twenge from San Diego State University, 80% of American high school seniors consider themselves as being "very important." This is compared to just 12% thinking so in a similar survey conducted in the 50s.[67] I can only imagine what the percentage would be if they surveyed Wall Street professionals today! The problem with a large ego is that it taints self-examination. Most of us are biased towards thinking of ourselves as better than we really are. Therefore, any serious effort towards becoming more self-aware requires constant feedback from less biased people.

Put Yourself in an Environment Conducive to Self-Examination

The best organization cultures are those that encourage objective feedback and where people feel less need to be defensive towards negative feedback. Junior people often benefit significantly when senior members of the firm are held accountable for their professional development. However, there are other times, especially for those that have already built up a significant amount of expertise, when it may make more sense to not have someone else constantly watching over you. For example, when Stanley Druckenmiller first joined Soros Fund Management as a young man, he initially struggled under the direct oversight of his idol. It is hard enough to be self-aware. It can be exponentially more difficult to invest trying to also be aware of your boss' various personality traits, motivations, emotional biases, etc. The partnership between Soros and Druckenmiller flourished only after the young star convinced the older legend that the firm would be better off if Soros became less involved with day to day investing decisions. Instead of micro-managing, George Soros evolved into a person Druckenmiller would go to for advice. As Soros focused more on his philanthropy, Druckenmiller became increasingly free to experiment. Instead of wasting a lot of energy trying to guess how his boss would react, he spent more time learning about himself and how he would react if certain dynamics changed in the market. Druckenmiller's experience illustrates how one needs to sometimes be proactive in shaping his or her environment

Take Assessment Tests

Another way to conduct self-examination in an objective way is to take assessment tests. Many tests can be found on the Internet and many decent ones are actually free. I learned more about my personality traits after taking Dr. Richard Peterson's free test, which can be found at:

www.marketpsych.com/personality_test.php

Travis Bradberry also provides a good quick test with the purchase of his book, *Emotional Intelligence 2.0,* which scores your current state of self / social awareness and other aspects of emotional intelligence.

Examine Motivations

From time to time, it can be helpful to ask yourself why you want to do what you are currently doing. This exercise also can stop you from making some mistakes. For example, I have realized that I have a tendency to seek excitement. This propensity sometimes clouds my analysis. I take on more risk than I otherwise should. Simply stopping once in a while to reflect on the fact that I was seeking a thrill has saved me from making many bad investment decisions.

Stop Judging Emotions

According to legendary investor Ed Seykota, "If running out of gas is a bad feeling, you might be tempted to put masking tape over your fuel gauge... and miss out on the positive intention of that information."[68] In order to learn from our emotions, we should try to accept our feelings for what they are. Describing a specific emotion as "bad" can lead to ignoring what the emotion may be telling you. It can also lead to a fear of feeling the emotion at all.

Take Inventory of Your Mood

Since your mood can have an impact on the amount of risk you are willing to take, it is important to understand what your mood currently is like. This can be done in a journal on a daily basis or by asking colleagues that know you well to point out to you when your mood seems to be at a relative high or low. Whenever my portfolio does well for several days or weeks in a row, I make it a point to reflect on my mood. I do not want to let the recent success lead to complacency.

Seek Out the Source of Your Feelings

Self-reflection involves trying to understand why you are feeling the way you are. This is not easy, but it mainly just involves some quiet time to think. As you will learn in the next part of the book, it is likely that others are feeling the same way you are. Putting in the time to understand the source of your emotions can bring about an investing edge. For example, if a negative development occurs and I realize that my investment thesis is wrong, I may feel shame in selling at a slight loss. Feeling shame is good. It tells me that I am holding an investment for the wrong reasons. Moreover, it actually gives me the courage to quickly exit the bad investment. By selling quickly, I lose less money than others who are more dismissive of what their feelings might be telling them.

PART 2

SOCIAL AWARENESS

CHAPTER 7

Gaining an Edge through Empathy

"To distinguish yourself from others, you need to be on the right side of those mistakes." – Howard Marks, *The Most Important Thing*

Empathy is the ability to put oneself in another person's shoes and feel what they are going through. It is why we cry when we watch sad movies. It is why we feel exhilaration when our favorite tennis player comes from behind to win a match. It is why babies often smile at us after we smile at them. Empathy is at the heart of morality across virtually every religion. Adam Smith was one of the first Western writers to discuss empathy as the foundation for kindhearted action. He stated, "When we see a stroke aimed and just ready to fall upon the leg or arm of another person, we naturally shrink and draw back our leg or our own arm; and when it does fall, we feel it in some measure, and are hurt by it as well as the sufferer."[69]

Over the last several years, a tremendous amount of scientific research has been conducted to understand the sources of empathy. Scientists have identified a type of neuron in the brain that is largely responsible for it. These so-called "mirror neurons" have been shown to fire while just watching other people. For example, when you see someone smile, your mirror neurons respond and they even cause some of the muscles in your face to move slightly. Brain scans demonstrate that when you see, hear or think about other people in pain, many of the same regions of the brain are activated as when you experience pain yourself. Our mirror neurons act as sort of wireless data receivers. They help us tap into the emotions of others. All it takes is for us to look, listen or even just think about what others are going through.

Daniel Goleman identifies three types of empathy: cognitive empathy, emotional empathy and empathetic concern. Cognitive empathy helps us understand the perspective of others. If you are bearish on a particular investment, you use this form of empathy to understand how someone who is bullish thinks. We use cognitive empathy to better understand the other side of our investments; thereby, either gaining more conviction that we are right or realizing that we are wrong. Emotional empathy allows you to feel with others. Investors who have high emotional empathy are able to identify with the sentiment of the market and take advantage of the emotional biases of others. For example, Stanley Druckenmiller bought equities aggressively before the 1991 Gulf war started. He sensed that most other participants in the market were feeling nervous. He realized that they preferred to wait for the war before actually commencing their buying. Therefore, by being empathetic to the nervousness felt by others, Druckenmiller was able to buy ahead of them. Another form of emotional empathy is when one recognizes that one's own emotions are similar to most others in the marketplace. For example, Mark Cook, the famous day trader profiled in *Stock Market Wizards*, says that he uses his own fear to know when the right time to buy is. He knows that when he is feeling very scared, most others in the market are also likely feeling at least as scared as him. Empathetic concern is what we typically describe as compassion. Those with strong empathetic concern are good at sensing what others need. For example, traders who have high empathetic concern, can sense when others may be desperate for liquidity. In *More Money than God*, Paul Tudor Jones is described as someone that would score highly in empathetic concern. He often understands when others in the market are forced to sell. Jones is able to empathize with a wide range of people from the Japanese fund managers facing employment risk due to underperformance to the American cotton farmer desperate to sell in December for tax purposes. In fact, many of his big winning trades that have been written about seem to be almost entirely explained by his superior level of empathetic concern.

To empathize is an extremely powerful capability of the brain. Not utilizing empathy while investing is a terrible waste of mental resources. Nevertheless, most text books on investing spend almost no time on it. Instead, they focus almost entirely on quantifiable items that are easy to analyze. The problem with things that are easy to quantify and analyze is that computers can generally do that much better and quicker than humans. Consequently, the investor can have difficulty ever gaining a competitive advantage by just employing traditional security analysis. The great thing about empathy is that we are all born with it. Infants have been shown to imitate facial expressions of those in front of them almost immediately after birth. The easiest way to gain an investing edge by employing our God-given capacity to empathize is to simply ask yourself what others in the marketplace may be feeling. You should try to understand what the current shareholders and potential buyers of a particular security are thinking before you make any investment decision. Before making an investment, I ask myself 7 questions:

1. What does the current shareholder base look like? Is it mostly comprised of value investors who usually bet against the current momentum and take a longer term perspective, or growth and shorter term investors who typically sell after poor results? Is there a high short interest? Does management own a large percentage?
2. What are the longer term shareholders thinking and feeling?
3. What are the shareholders who recently bought the stock thinking and feeling?
4. What is the potential buyer of the stock thinking and feeling?
5. What is the potential short seller of the stock thinking and feeling?

6. If the stock has a high short interest, what are those who are already short the stock thinking and feeling?
7. What is management thinking and feeling?

Answering these questions allows you to develop an investing edge through empathy. As you will see in the next chapter, technical analysis can be a great tool. However, these questions can also be answered in many ways including looking at investor surveys, examining questions that are asked by financial analysts on company conference calls, questioning management, examining changes in the shareholder base and conversing with other investors.

Below, I give three real life examples. In the first example, I describe how successfully answering these questions led me to have conviction to successfully sell short a stock in the aftermarket immediately after the company reported its quarterly earnings. In the second example, I show how answering these questions saved me from making a costly mistake. In the third example, I reveal how developing an empathetic edge helped me to gain conviction to buy a stock.

Using Empathy: Example #1

This example is based on the following Research in Motion (RIMM) stock chart.

Figure 2: RIMM on September 15, 2011

Shares of Research in Motion (RIMM) had been performing very poorly well before September 15, 2011. The company missed a revolutionary change in the smartphone industry. Instead of investing in touch-screen technology and developing an ecosystem for application developers, RIMM continued to focus mostly on messaging and making phones with physical keyboards and relatively small screens. As a result, Apple's iPhone and phones based on Google's Android operating system were steadily taking market share away from the company. It seemed obvious the trend would continue, since RIMM would likely not be able to catch up even if it drastically changed its research and development focus. Therefore, RIMM was a stock that had a clear negative trend. I had been short RIMM in 2010. I also took profits too early in 2011— I had fallen victim to my bias of recognizing my winners too early. Recognizing my mistake, I wanted to re-short RIMM, but several good sell-side research analysts, like Ehud Gelblum at Morgan Stanley, had been talking about how they expected the company to report relatively strong results for the quarter. They had various

95

reasons for why the results may look good in the short term. The rationale seemed to make sense, so I decided to wait until after the company reported quarterly results to reevaluate whether to short RIMM or not. When the company reported earnings on September 15, 2011, it turned out that the analysts were wrong. The company missed expectations and also gave weak guidance for the following quarter. The stock started to trade down in the aftermarket and I immediately developed an empathetic edge that gave me the conviction to short RIMM's stock even after it was already down 6% in the aftermarket. I asked myself the following questions:

1. What did the shareholder base look like? When I looked at the largest holders of the stock on Bloomberg (individual investors can obtain this information from sites like Yahoo! Finance), I recognized many growth investors. I did not see many shareholders that describe themselves as value investors, who typically "fight the momentum of the pendulum." Furthermore, the sell-side research analysts talking about potential positive short term results probably got several short term traders involved. These shareholders were hoping to make a quick buck by selling after the positive results were released. The stock also had a relatively high short interest.

2. What were the longer term shareholders thinking and feeling? Since many of the shareholders were institutions that typically invest use a growth investing approach. I knew that many would be reluctant to add to their positions after a "miss." I also understood that most of the longer term shareholders felt stuck in money-losing positions. Many of these holders were probably hoping to get back to breakeven. They feared locking in a loss. They didn't want to feel the shame that comes from being proven wrong. People typically act like this until the losses and pain become

96

too great. I realized that the earnings miss by RIMM could make many of these shareholders capitulate. By putting myself in their shoes, I also recognized that many of these institutions probably wouldn't want to answer questions from their clients regarding why they still owned RIMM. Most institutions have to report their holdings every quarter. Since RIMM reported close to the end of the September quarter, I understood that many of these shareholders would have an incentive to dump their position over the next couple of weeks.

3. What were the shareholders who recently bought the stock, thinking and feeling? As described above, the positive financial analyst commentary regarding short term business conditions probably attracted some short term buyers. These buyers were hoping for a short term bounce in the shares following the results. Some of these buyers already had significant gains, because in the 5 weeks leading up to RIMM's results the stock went up over 30%. Putting myself in their shoes, I recognized that many would immediately want to sell after the disappointing results. They were wrong on the fundamentals, yet with the stock only down 6% in the aftermarket, many of these holders still had a significant gain. They would want to lock-in that gain now that the event they were waiting for had passed. They feared feeling the regret that would come if their winner became a loser.

4. What was the potential buyer of the stock thinking and feeling? The potential buyer of RIMM's stock was the value buyer that bets against momentum. Putting myself in his shoes, I would probably wait for lower prices before buying the stock. I would certainly not want to rush to buy the stock in the aftermarket. Furthermore, since the company's market share in the smartphone market appeared to now be

declining at an accelerating rate, I would be in no rush to build a meaningful position. An investor who prefers contesting momentum knows to be careful with initial position sizing. In the immediate future, he is likely to lose money as the momentum continues in its current direction.

5.   What was the potential short seller of the stock thinking and feeling? This was the easiest question for me to answer. I had a long term negative view on the company, but was scared to get involved because of what some analysts were saying regarding RIMM's business in the short term. Once the quarter's results were out and business turned out to be bad, I felt regret for not being involved already and did not want to feel even more regret if the stock continued to go lower. I wanted to re-short the stock as long as I could still short it at a reasonable price and I recognized that there were probably many others thinking like me.

6.   If the stock has a high short interest, what were those who were already short the stock thinking and feeling? While the short interest was relatively high, the commentary from the sell-side analysts likely caused some of the people who were short the stock to cover at least a portion of their positions ahead of the earnings call. They had gains and did not want to risk losing them. Like me, these people were waiting until after the quarter to short more RIMM stock. While they were wrong to cover their shorts, many of these people felt lucky since they most probably covered their positions over the last month at prices that were still lower than where the stock was trading in the aftermarket.

7.   What is management thinking and feeling?   On the conference call, management appeared to be finally facing reality. In the past, they seemed to be arrogant and in denial of market share trends. They felt that their new products

would help them come back on top. There was a clear attitude shift on this call. For example, Co-CEO James Balsillie initiated the quarterly conference call by saying, "The last few quarters have been some of the most trying in the recent history of this Company." He also said, "We recognize that our shareholders may feel we have fallen short in terms of product execution, market share and financial performance." While it is always better for management to be fully aware of their current situation, this attitude shift did not change my negative bias towards the stock. Any improvement in RIMM's revenue performance would require significant investments that would reduce profitability. Management finally recognizing their predicament meant that consensus earnings estimates, at least for the next year or so, would have to fall further.

After synthesizing the answers to all these questions, it became clear to me that the stock needed to go much lower than just 6% after these disappointing results. The weak financial performance would influence many of the longer term holders to capitulate, especially since not doing so by the end of September would require them to have to answer questions from their clients. Most of the shorter term holders would sell since they didn't get what they hoped for. Furthermore, many of them actually had gains that they would want to try to realize quickly. Those who were short, and who covered their positions at lower prices, felt lucky to have been wrong on the fundamentals but to still have an opportunity to re-short at a higher price than where they covered. The potential value buyer would be very cautious buying the stock given the rapidly declining market share.

Using Empathy: Example #2

This example is based on the following Nokia (NOK) stock chart.

Figure 3: NOK on December 19, 2011

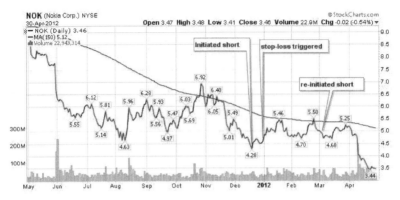

In December 2011, Nokia (NOK) had a lot of fundamental similarities to Research in Motion. Both had missed the technology shift towards touch-screens and applications in the smartphone industry. Both were losing market share. Both stocks seemed to be trending in a downward pattern. I shorted Nokia's stock on December 19, 2011. However, after the stock quickly shot up 10%, I stuck to my rule of using a stop-loss whenever I have a losing position in a security where a momentum investing approach should be applied. Recall that I am only willing to take large percentage losses on stocks when I am making highly contrarian bets. After I realized the loss on my Nokia position, I reflected on what went wrong and immediately realized that I did not try to develop an empathetic edge. If I did, I would have realized that while Nokia and RIMM had many similarities, they also had many differences with respect to how their current and potential shareholders were thinking and feeling. While RIMM's largest shareholders were growth investors, NOK's shareholder base comprised mostly value investors such as Dodge & Cox. These investors were less inclined to sell after bad news. Furthermore, while RIMM probably had many short term buyers that were hoping for a good quarter, Nokia did not seem to have many shareholders looking for a short term bounce. Some of the sell-side financial analysts were hopeful about RIMM experiencing strong short term business conditions; however, most analysts were relatively negative regarding NOK. Recall in the 5 weeks prior to RIMM's earnings announcement on September, 2011, RIMM's stock was up over 30%. NOK's stock was actually *down* over 30% in the 5 weeks before I initiated my short position. Most importantly, if I had put myself in the shoes of a current shareholder or someone already bearishly positioned towards NOK, I would have probably thought more about the annual Consumer Electronics Show (CES) in Las Vegas in January and 3GSM conference in Barcelona in February. Unlike RIMM, Nokia had a change in leadership and was not in denial of its competitive situation. In March 2011, NOK hired a new CEO who came from outside the company. Current holders and potential buyers of the stock were hoping to see better, more competitive products from Nokia. The company gives a preview of its new products at CES and 3GSM every year. Therefore, by putting myself in the shoes of a typical shareholder of Nokia stock that had a money-losing position, I would have not wanted to realize a loss until I read reviews of these new Nokia products. Someone who had been short NOK for some time and who had a large unrealized gain would probably have felt the urge to cover ahead of CES. The short seller would have feared losing his gain, if NOK did, in fact, come out with more competitive products. After going through this empathetic process, it seemed obvious that NOK's stock would rally as shorts covered ahead of the CES event.

While I lost money on my trade in Nokia, I think of the loss as payment for a valuable lesson. I learned that it is important to always try to develop an empathetic edge no matter how good or bad I think a company's fundamentals are. Reflecting on my loss also gave me the courage to take another shot with shorting NOK in March 2012 when I saw that NOK did not showcase any new exciting products at the CES or 3GSM conferences. I realized that the current shareholders could start to give up hope on the company's turnaround. After the company reported weak quarterly results in April 2012, the stock dropped significantly. I wound up making much more money with my second short trade in Nokia stock than I lost the first time around.

Using Empathy: Example #3

This example is based on the following eBay (EBAY) stock chart.

Figure 4: EBAY on March 7, 2012

In March 2012, my gut instinct led me to evaluate buying shares of eBay (EBAY). eBay's PayPal division had been growing rapidly and had recently entered a new and very large market. PayPal's main business had been to provide payment and settlement services to consumers and merchants that did business over the Internet. The change was that PayPal had started to offer similar services to traditional "offline" retail. While it was unclear how successful PayPal would eventually be away from the Internet, it was evident that any success in this much larger market had the potential to significantly positively impact eBay's earnings profile and growth potential. I followed my process to develop an empathetic edge:

1. What did the current shareholder base look like? When I looked at the largest holders, I saw a fair amount of value investors. Dodge & Cox was a large holder and so were several hedge funds that described themselves as value investors. There also were some growth investors. For over a year before I invested in March 2012, EBAY fluctuated from the high 20s to the low 30s. While the stock was relatively stable during that time, value investors still felt like they were betting against momentum since the stock was becoming cheaper. 2011 Earnings per share grew 17% from $1.73 to $2.03 and was expected to grow again in 2012. Therefore, since the stock had not really moved, the stock's price-to-earnings ratio had declined. The growth investors who were involved were focusing on eBay's PayPal business, which had been experiencing rapid growth. eBay's founder also still held a relatively large stake, which was very unlikely to be sold rapidly. The short interest did not stand out as very high or low.

2. What were the longer term shareholders thinking and feeling? By the time I was looking to invest, EBAY was close to $36. Therefore, everyone who had bought it over the last 15 months between the high 20s and the low 30s made a profit. Some of the value investors were probably looking to book a quick profit and exit. However, because of my understanding of association bias, I understood that they would want to buy more stock if EBAY fell back close to the price at which they originally bought. Many of the growth investors that were involved probably saw the improvement in eBay's stock as confirmation of their thesis. Therefore,

some of the growth investors were likely looking to buy more.

3. What were the shareholders who recently bought the stock, thinking and feeling? Shareholders who recently bought were most likely growth or momentum investors since, for the first time in a while, EBAY started to look to have a positive upward trend. However, these new shareholders were probably cautious of building too big a position. They would be looking to add to their positions if the trend and fundamentals looked like they would continue improving.

4. What was the potential buyer of the stock thinking and feeling? This was the easiest question because I was the potential buyer. I was getting increasingly excited about the prospects for the PayPal business. I had seen other businesses that benefited tremendously when a large new addressable market opened up. The fact that the stock was in a relatively tight range over the past year also gave me some comfort of the downside risk. I thought to myself: "When nobody really thought about the offline retail market as a large opportunity for PayPal, the stock hovered around $31. Now that this huge new market potential has emerged, it most probably won't go much below that level, if at all." Consequently, with the stock at $36, I was able to quantify my downside risk to be about $5. However, since I had done some fundamental analysis on where EBAY could go if PayPal had success in offline retail, I realized that the upside potential far outweighed the downside risk.

5. What was the potential short seller of the stock thinking and feeling? I couldn't see how a short seller would be interested in EBAY. The stock was not expensive, earnings were growing, and if PayPal was successful in offline retail, the upside in earnings power would be tremendous. The risk /

reward did not seem to make sense for a short seller. Even if PayPal would be a failure in offline retail, there would be no way for anyone to develop a strong view regarding that for quite a long time.

6. What was management thinking and feeling? The company had some turnover in management over the last few years. New management probably felt pressure to deliver good results, especially given the lack of performance in eBay's stock over the last year.

After amalgamating the answers to all these questions, I felt like I had an empathetic edge. While some value investors would sell to lock-in profits, growth investors would likely buy given the potential of PayPal and the fact that eBay's stock finally started to exhibit some positive momentum. Furthermore, because of association bias, it was probable that most of the value investors that did sell would look to buy back on weakness. Therefore, I didn't think the investment carried significant risk. Even if PayPal would be a failure in offline retail, that would not be known for at least another year or two, so there was no great reason for a growth investor to sell or for a short seller to get involved. Unless something changed very significantly for the worse, the stock seemed much more likely to go up than down.

CHAPTER 8

Demystifying Technical Analysis

"It is very important for me to study the details of price action to see if I can observe something about how everybody is voting. Studying the charts is absolutely crucial and alerts me to existing disequilibria and potential changes." - Bruce Kovner, *Market Wizards*

In this chapter, I demonstrate why technical analysis (chart reading) can be helpful to most, if not all, types of investors. Technical analysis works because it takes account of investor psychology. A chart can tell you a tremendous amount about what the current shareholders of a security may be feeling. It can be a visual manifestation of many of the biases discussed in Chapter 3. Let me begin by telling the story of how I discovered chart reading.

When I started investing in the public markets, I thought that analyzing charts was a complete waste of time. At Wharton, I learned about how a company's market valuation was theoretically based on the present value of the free cash flow it would generate for shareholders over time. We learned almost nothing about how a stock's historical pattern can be indicative of future performance. I tended to view stock market technicians as almost like astrologers or witch doctors. They talked in a vocabulary that seemed foreign. They talked about things such as the "inverse head and shoulders pattern" and "ascending triangles." One word the technicians loved to say was "breakout." I learned that this was when a stock made a new high or went above what the chartist believed to be a strong resistance level. Most technicians recommended buying after a stock "broke out." I did not understand this. Weren't we supposed to buy low and sell high? Why were these technicians recommending people to buy stocks that just made new highs? They were also telling people to sell stocks that made new lows. Finally, many technicians saw different patterns when looking at the same charts. This often led them to have conflicting recommendations. In *A Random Walk Down Wall Street*, Burton Malkiel affirmed, "Under scrutiny, chart-reading must share a pedestal with alchemy."[70] It all seemed to make no sense.

I originally dismissed trying to learn anything about reading charts, but that started to change. I read books like *Market Wizards* and saw that many of the greatest investors actually heavily relied on technical analysis. I also started noticing that some of the best known technicians that worked at sell-side brokerage firms appeared to be right much more often than not. They seemed to be especially prescient in calling turns in the overall market. For example, many technicians turned bearish in 2000 and in 2007 well before it became clear the economy's fundamentals were significantly weakening. Andrew Lo, a finance professor at MIT, argues that academic research of some of the rules behind technical analysis and statistical studies of the buy / sell recommendations of certain chartists appears to validate the role of chart reading. In *The Evolution of Technical Analysis*, Lo and co-author Jasmina Hasanhodzic state, "Certain technical patterns, when applied to many stocks over many time periods, do provide incremental information, especially for Nasdaq stocks, supporting the claim that technical analysis can add incremental value to the investment process."[71] Suddenly, I saw technical analysis as a competency I needed to learn in order to be a better investor.

Most technicians who write about their methodologies think that people should follow them just because of the results. They spend very little time explaining *why* chart reading seems to work. I believe that a stock's chart aids in developing an investing edge through empathy. It can help answer some or all of the questions listed in the previous chapter, especially those questions that deal with how the current shareholders are feeling.

Chart reading can be considered more art than science and technicians vary greatly in their techniques. However, there are certain principles that virtually every technician will agree with. 10 of them are listed below. Each principle is followed by an explanation for why the rule makes sense from an empathetic perspective:

Technical Analysis: Principle #1

A resistance level is a level at which, all other things being equal, the price is more likely to fall than rise, because it meets *resistance* in the market.

Figure 5

The chart above is of Apple (AAPL) stock from 2001 to 2003. It is an example of a chart that formed a resistance level. The stock spent a fair amount of 2001 and the first half of 2002 trading in a range from about $11 to $13. During the summer of 2002, Apple's stock then suddenly declined. Let's put ourselves in the shoes of an average shareholder in early 2003 when the stock was at $7. These shareholders were sitting on paper losses. Many acquired the stock over the last couple of years at prices that were higher. They were hoping for a bounce in the stock, so that they could sell and potentially have a break-even result or a slight gain. That way, they could avoid the shame that comes from being wrong. Since many bought slightly under $13 - that would be about the same price they would sell. This intention for many shareholders to sell at a certain price creates a resistance level. When the stock moved up towards the end of 2003, many of these shareholders unloaded their positions and the stock failed to get past $13 again. The more time a stock spends churning near the resistance level, the stronger the level tends to be. This is because new shareholders have an average cost basis near resistance. Therefore, duration and trading volume near resistance impacts how strong the level is. The number of times the resistance level has been successfully tested also is important. This is because traders who short the stock near resistance experience a positive outcome with their decision if the stock drops back down. Because of the association bias, they become more inclined to re-short the stock again if it gets close to resistance. Please note that I am not advocating blindly shorting stocks that are close to resistance. I am trying to explain why the concept of resistance makes sense. I do not advocate making investment decisions based solely on the chart. In fact, if your intuition and fundamental analysis suggest reasons for a break past resistance, it may actually be best to *buy* slightly below this level as explained in principle #2 below.

Technical Analysis: Principle #2

Stocks should be bought when they break out of strong resistance levels, especially when the breakout is accompanied by high volume and / or overly negative sentiment. When a stock breaks out above resistance, the old resistance level becomes a support level.

Figure 6

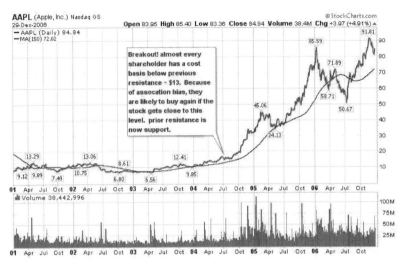

Let's now look at Apple's stock chart by adding an additional 3 years after 2003. AAPL is an example of a stock that broke out of a strong resistance level. Because a lot of time went by with the stock trading in a narrow range between about $7 and $13 from 2001 to 2003, a strong resistance level was created. Churn in the shareholder base created many shareholders whose average cost was slightly below $13. In the middle of 2004, the stock rapidly broke that resistance level with strong volume. Usually, this happens when something fundamentally changes. In this case, Apple's brand was reinvigorated by new products. Steve Jobs had returned as CEO and the changes he instituted improved the company's growth prospects and competitive positioning. Now put yourself in the shoes of all those Apple shareholders who had bought slightly below $13. At the time of the breakout in 2004, many of them had gains. Some decided to sell and realize a profit. However, because they associated a positive outcome with buying near $13, they likely would have looked to buy the stock back if it got back close to that price. Resistance became support. After the breakout in 2004, the stock became more probable to go higher than to go lower and break support. This is the type of chart pattern that you would much rather have if you are looking to buy a stock, and a pattern you should avoid if you are looking to short a stock. Notice how volume for Apple's shares increased around the time of the breakout and continued to increase through the beginning of 2005. The more trading volume that accompanies a breakout, the better the chance is that a stock will go higher. More trading volume means more new shareholders, who are created with an average cost basis higher than the old resistance level. These shareholders are going to be slow to sell if the stock drifts back down. More trading volume also means that many of the older shareholders, who had their average cost near the old resistance level, sold at a profit. They are likely to buy back the stock if it drifts lower. Generally, the stronger the resistance level was, the stronger the support level will be. This is because there are more shareholders with a positive association bias. Furthermore, the more negative the market's sentiment is regarding a stock, the better the chances are that the stock will go higher. A market that is highly skeptical about a breakout has more potential buyers than sellers. In *Market Wizards*, Bruce Kovner said, "If everybody believes there is no reason for corn to breakout, and it suddenly does, the chances that there is an important underlying cause are much greater." The most common ways to measure sentiment are to look at its short interest, sell-side analyst ratings or simply by looking at the stock's performance.

Technical Analysis: Principle #3

A support level is a level at which, all other things being equal, the price is more likely to rise than fall, because it finds *support* in the market.

Figure 7

The chart above is of Yahoo (YHOO) stock from late 2004 to mid-2006. It is an example of a chart that created a support level. During this time period, the stock approached $30 many times. Each time it did so, it quickly bounced up. Anyone who bought Yahoo's stock near $30 during this time period experienced a quick payoff. We know that successful outcomes lead to association biases. After experiencing a positive outcome buying near $30, people are more inclined to mindlessly buy the same stock again whenever it approaches $30. The intention of many shareholders to buy near a certain price creates a support level. As you can see, the support level became very apparent during the first half of 2006. During this time, shareholders bought the stock over and over again whenever it approached $30. The more often the stock bounces off the support level, the stronger people's association bias is. Therefore, duration and trading volume at support impacts how strong the level tends to be. The number of times the support level has been successfully tested is also important. As with resistance levels, please note that I am not advocating blindly buying stocks that are close to support. I am trying to explain why the concept of support makes sense. I do not advocate making investment decisions based solely on the chart. In fact, if your intuition and fundamental analysis suggest reasons for a break below the support level, it may be actually best to *short* the stock above this level as explained in principle #4 below.

Technical Analysis: Principle #4

Stocks should be sold when they break through strong support levels, especially when the breakdown is accompanied by high volume and / or overly positive sentiment. When a stock breaks through a support level, the former support level becomes a resistance level.

Figure 8

Like we did with Apple, lets add a few years to Yahoo's stock chart. The above chart is an example of a breakdown. After holding the $30 support level for a couple of years, YHOO dropped to $25 in July 2006. Let's put ourselves in the shoes of all those people that bought the stock above $30. When the stock went to $25, each of these shareholders had a money-losing investment. Most of us find it very difficult to admit to ourselves or to others that we are wrong. We know this creates a bias to hold losing positions too long. Many of these people were hoping for the stock to go back up above $30. They strongly wanted to sell the stock for a break-even result or for a slight gain; thereby, they could avoid any shame for being wrong. This is how a resistance level is created. The previous support level became resistance. All other things being equal, the stock will now have a more difficult time getting past $30 than it will of going down further. We know that as the stock approaches $30, it will face a large amount of selling pressure from all those shareholders who previously bought near that price. This is exactly what happened. Note how every time the stock rallied in 2007 and 2008, the upturn fizzled near $30. This is the type of chart pattern you prefer to see when you are short a stock and not when you are long. The more time a stock spends churning at resistance, the more shareholders are created that have an average cost near the resistance level. Therefore, duration and trading volume at the resistance level impacts how strong the level tends to be. After failing to break through the $30 resistance level several times, YHOO dropped significantly at the end of 2008.

Technical Analysis: Principle #5

A stock making higher highs and higher lows is more likely to go up than a stock making lower highs and lower lows.

Figure 9

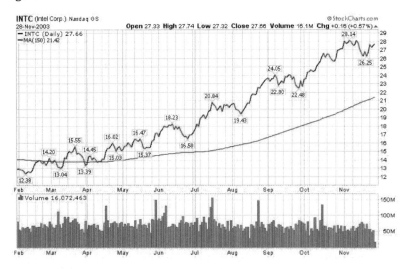

The chart of Intel (INTC) stock in 2003 is an example of a stock making higher highs and higher lows. This is considered a healthy pattern. As the stock goes up, some investors sell to realize gains, but many have associated a positive enough bias to buy back the stock at prices slightly higher than where they originally bought it. Furthermore, as the stock rises, new buyers come in. The stock may have mostly had value investors that were "fighting the momentum" before the stock broke out. As a stock continues making higher highs and higher lows, the shareholder base gradually transitions to be more growth oriented investors who expect current trends benefiting the company to continue or even accelerate.

Technical Analysis: Principle #6

Bull markets tend to top out when market breadth declines. Market breadth can be defined as the number of stocks in the market making new highs. Similarly, bear markets tend to bottom out when there is a declining number of stocks making new lows.

THE EMOTIONALLY INTELLIGENT INVESTOR

Recall from Chapter 3 that one of the biases many people have is that they are overly focused on a win / loss ratio. A win / loss ratio does not make analytic sense, because one could have a portfolio with 9 losers and 1 winner and still make a lot of money as long as the winner was sized bigger and / or had a much better return. Nevertheless, a win / loss ratio tends to impact people's happiness. When people see a lot of their investments down, they tend to become less happy even if they are still making money. We know that sadness leads to increased risk aversion. Increased risk aversion from an environment that was previously risk-seeking is what leads to bear markets.

Technical Analysis: Principle #7

Bull markets tend to top out when the leading group of stocks start underperforming.

The leading group of stocks is the collection of securities that outperform during a bull market. In 1999, the Internet sector was the leading group. Many mutual fund investors went from being under-exposed to technology stocks in the early 1990s to being heavily overweight them in the late 1990s. When the Internet sector started to underperform in early 2000, it was a sign that the bull market had ended. The average investor that heavily owned these stocks started underperforming. This caused the average investor to be sad, which resulted in risk aversion. As stated above, a negative change from the average investor's appetite for risk taking is what leads to bear markets.

Technical Analysis: Principle #8

The end of bull markets and the end of bear moves often have one last big move up and down, respectively.

Figure 10

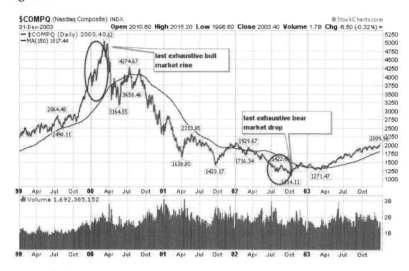

In *A Gift to My Children*, Jim Rogers states, "Charts sometimes reveal a B-line rise – an indication that prices have increased far beyond actual value. It means that people have lost perspective. It shows the level of hysteria."[72] There are several human biases that lead to a final exhaustive rally in any bubble. Positive investment returns make us happy and we know that happiness leads us to become more risk-seeking. We also know that we have a tendency to become overconfident. Finally, we have an inclination to herd. All these biases are factors that inflate a bubble. In 1999, people bought Internet stocks, which caused the stocks to go up, which caused people to be more confident in buying other "dot com" stocks. Their friends and neighbors also started buying Internet stocks, because they did not want to miss out. They were all happy with making money. The improved mood caused them to make ever more impulsive and riskier investment decisions. People became so confident that they did not care about traditional factors like earnings. Instead, they thought they could accurately predict what fast-changing companies would look like in 20 years. The reinforcing cycle caused mass hysteria, which led to rapidly rising stock

118

prices. At the end of a bear market, the opposite reinforcing cycle happens. People lose money, which causes them to be sad, which causes them to take less risk. They become less confident and become overly concerned about low probability risks. They spend very little time thinking about positive outcomes. The chart above shows the Nasdaq Composite Index from 1999 to 2003. At the end of 1999 and the beginning of 2000, the "dotcom" bubble ended with an explosive rally. The bear market that followed did not end until a final exhaustive drop at the end of 2002.

Technical Analysis: Principle #9

Stock prices tend to go down much faster than they go up.

Figure 11

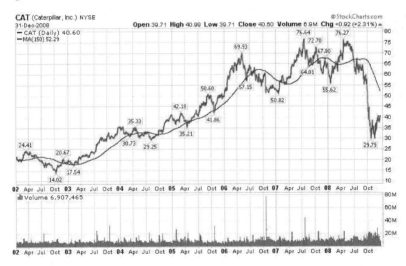

The above chart of Caterpillar (CAT) stock from 2002 to 2008 is an example of a cyclical stock that people became enthusiastic about and then subsequently sold in a panic. Notice how the stock steadily rose from the end of 2002 to the beginning of 2008 and then gave up a substantial portion of those gains in less than a few months. People generally feel twice as much sadness or pain when something is lost than when something of equal value is gained. This is the main reason why stocks go down faster than they go up. People tend to get depressed and want to capitulate much faster than the time it takes for them to get euphoric. Furthermore, as a stock rises, many people quickly sell to lock-in their gains. The shareholder base gradually transitions from distressed and value investors, who contest the momentum of the metaphorical pendulum, to growth and momentum investors, who typically invest hoping to ride a trend. When a stock goes down and the pendulum's direction shifts, the only people that would be interested are the distressed or value investors. Since these types of investors tend to be less impulsive and generally more risk averse, they are usually slow to accumulate shares. After all, they know that betting against a current trend often results in initial losses. Distressed or value investors are in no rush to build fully-sized positions.

Technical Analysis: Principle #10

Short term overbought / oversold indicators help with timing. One should avoid initiating a full long position in a stock that has recently had a large up move, which would make it technically overbought. Similarly, one should avoid initiating a full short position in a stock that has recently had a large down move, which would make it technically oversold.

Figure 12

When a stock spikes up, put yourself in the shoes of the current shareholders. Many will want to realize gains and lock-in being right. Something may have fundamentally changed that makes the stock a good investment, but it is often prudent to not buy a maximum size position when a stock has recently increased significantly in a short period of time. All other things being equal, a stock that is very overbought in the short term will have some natural selling pressure that may take it down. The opposite is true of a stock that is much oversold. Chartists use many indicators to understand how overbought or oversold a particular stock is. One of the most common is the Relative Strength Index (RSI). A RSI of greater than 70 is usually considered overbought. A RSI of 30 or below ordinarily indicates that the stock is technically oversold. Recall from the previous chapter about how I mistakenly shorted Nokia's stock in December 2011 without developing an edge through empathy. As the chart above demonstrates, NOK was technically oversold when I sold it short. If I had looked at the RSI indicator, I would have probably avoided initiating a fully-sized position right away and would have limited the loss on that mistake.

There is some disagreement between technicians on the importance of volume and timeframe. Some do not look much at the volume traded to determine a support level. Other technicians think that a resistance level created 5 years ago is just as strong as one created last year. I believe trading volume must be considered when reviewing charts. A support level where a lot of volume has traded is much more powerful than a support level created by light volume even if the latter was in place for a slightly longer period of time. This is because you have more shareholders who have built a positive association with the support level. Timeframe is also important. All other things being equal, I believe a stock has a higher likelihood of breaking out of a resistance level that was created 5 years ago than one that was created 1 year ago. Many of the people that bought the stock 5 years ago may have already sold. There would be less people waiting to get back to break-even. That being said, a resistance level that has been created *over* several years, and / or one that has been successfully tested over many years, can be more powerful than a level created a year ago.

Many chartists like to look at moving averages. For example, Stan Weinstein, a well-known technician, heavily relies upon the 150 day moving average in his analysis. He is usually negative on stocks that are trading below their 150 day moving average and when the moving average has a descending slope. Because the moving averages represent an average price over a given time period, they can be a shortcut to understanding what the average cost basis is for most of the shareholders who bought the stock during the time frame involved. Weinstein would argue that a stock trading below its 150 day moving average has many shareholders that are holding onto money-losing positions. The shareholders that bought the stock over the last 150 days are waiting to sell at a price that would yield a break-even result. It is likely that for many of them, this price is somewhere near the 150 day moving average. I believe using moving averages as a proxy for empathizing with the current cost basis of many shareholders makes sense in many cases. However, one must be careful about applying this rule blindly. We have to remember that moving averages are not actually the average price that was traded over a given period of time. This would only be theoretically correct if trading volume was exactly the same every day and if the stock didn't fluctuate throughout the day. Again, paying attention to trading volume allows one to better empathize with shareholders. A stock whose trading volume has significantly dried up over the last several months is not the same as a stock whose trading volume has been relatively consistent. The former is less likely to have as many shareholders with an average cost basis near the moving averages.

We learned in Chapter 3 how two of the most common emotional biases are to hold losing positions too long and to sell winning positions too early. We are inclined do so, because we fear feeling regret and shame. We sell our winners too quickly because we want to lock-in being right. We hold off on selling our losers in order to avoid (locking in) being wrong. These two biases are the foundation of technical analysis since they explain why resistance and support levels are created. As I have described above, many other principles of technical analysis can be explained through relating with people's common biases and vulnerabilities. Empathizing with other participants in the market is a key factor for developing conviction and an investing edge. Analyzing charts can aid tremendously in this effort.

CHAPTER 9

Using Social Awareness to Better Evaluate Corporate Management

"I try to get rid of people who always confidently answer questions about which they don't have any real knowledge." – Charlie Munger[73]

Social awareness involves more than empathy. People who are socially aware are good at listening and observing while they interact with others. They understand what others may be thinking and feeling, but they can also recognize group dynamics. They are good at quickly picking up on the mood of an organization, how the people within a given group are likely to behave with each other and whether people are trustworthy and self-aware. Dr. Travis Bradberry compares social awareness to anthropology. He states, "The difference is you won't be 100 yards away watching events unfold through a pair of binoculars. To be socially aware, you have to spot and understand people's emotions while you're right there in the middle of it – a contributing, yet astutely aware, member of the interaction."[74] In *Your Money and Your Brain,* Jason Zweig provides an example of how social awareness can help with investment decisions. Zweig mentions how Fred Kobrick, a mutual fund manager, reached out to shake hands with the CEO of a company in which he was seriously considering investing. Kobrick observed that the CEO had a distinctive monogram on his shirt cuff. Kobrick also noticed that other managers of the company had similar monograms. He got a bad feeling. Kobrick knew right then that he wouldn't want to make an investment in the company. He explained, "How could these guys ever bring bad news to the boss if they couldn't even think for themselves when they were buying shirts?"[75]

Familiarity with a company's incentive structure and with how its management historically reacts to questions can help with generating an investing edge using social awareness. For example, I once sat in a presentation by the CEO of an enterprise software company in which I was already invested. The Company had been performing poorly, so I had been using a value investing approach. The stock was trading at a very low valuation. I thought it was well below intrinsic value, especially if sales could start growing again. The presentation was made close to the end of the company's quarter. There were probably 200 people in the audience and it was webcasted, so anyone could listen in. The company had recently had recently overhauled most of its management and when asked by an audience member about the new team, the CEO *singled* out the new VP of sales as someone he thought was "fitting in nicely" I immediately felt even more confident in my investment. Most enterprise software companies book a relatively large chunk of their quarterly revenue in the last couple of weeks of the quarter. This is because salespeople get extra aggressive to make their quotas as the quarter comes to a close. Customers also know they can get discounts if they wait until salespeople are feeling more pressure to make quarterly quotas. The fact that the CEO talked positively about the new VP of sales so close to the end of the quarter told me that the business was most probably performing well. The CEO would almost certainly not have been complimentary about the new VP if bookings in the quarter were below plan. He didn't even have to bring up the VP of sales. He could have talked about other members of the team instead. Despite the fact that so many other investors listened to the CEO that day, most people seemed surprised when the company actually reported a good quarter just a few weeks later. In this case, I connected the CEO's comments with how people in the organization are incentivized to develop an edge that led me to have higher conviction in my investment. Knowledge of how management historically reacts to questions can also be helpful in developing an investing advantage through social awareness. For example, if a CFO of a company repeatedly comments on market rumors and then refuses to comment on a new story, it is highly possible that there is some truth to the latest gossip regarding the company.

There are many qualities that make an ideal management organization, but among the most important include self-awareness, trustworthiness, social awareness and the ability to execute. I have demonstrated why self-awareness is vital for investing success. It follows that since managers are constantly making investment decisions regarding company resources, they should also be self-aware. Managers who are trustworthy gain respect from their subordinates. As an investor you also take comfort knowing that management is not possibly hiding important negative information. Finally, every company needs leadership that sets ambitious goals and establishes incentives to ensure goals are achieved. Managers who are socially aware understand best how to do so, because they understand the motivations of their employees.

Many institutional investors will have the opportunity to meet face to face with management. This is one of the biggest advantages large investors have over individuals and smaller investors who cannot gain as much corporate access. In these meetings, it is important to pay as close attention as possible. Dr. Bradberry advises to not even take notes during meetings, because note-taking diverts attention from what needs to be observed. That advice may not be appropriate for everyone. Nevertheless, it is vital to remember that you are in the conversation to listen and learn something, not to wow the other person.[76] I often fall victim to thinking about my response or my next question while the other person is talking. It is hard enough to focus on someone else. It is much harder to listen to yourself at the same time. Not doing so may take practice. At least, it does for me. Very often, unadulterated observation results in emotional responses like the one Fred Kobrick had in the example above. Our brains will pick up on characteristics such as trustworthiness that we may not be able to articulate immediately. These gut feelings should not be dismissed just because they do not seem rational. A lot of communication is non-verbal. Our brains have evolved to recognize patterns, and when a person does something that seems inappropriate our brains generate negative emotional responses. A few examples of patterns that intuitively do not feel right include:

1. Facial expressions that do not match language. For example, OJ Simpson looked like he was smiling several times when he spoke about the murder of his ex-wife. Even though his words and tone of voice were appropriate, many people that watched him on TV came away with a negative feeling. His facial expressions did not seem to be in sync with his statements.

2. Communicators who do not maintain eye contact. In Western cultures, maintaining eye contact is expected. When someone looks away or closes his eyes while he is talking to you, it may be because he is afraid of looking directly at you while telling you a fabrication.

3. Nervous reactions. For most people, telling a lie induces stress. These emotions can be evinced when the person speaking shifts his weight to a different leg or if the person starts fiddling with small items in his reach.

4. Touching the face. Sometimes liars will cover their mouths while speaking to you. Touching the face is also an action that can indicate excess stress.

5. Eyes shifting in the wrong direction when answering questions involving the recall of information or images. When recalling information or what an image looks like, a right handed person will usually look up and to his

left. Looking up and to the right is done when one is trying to imagine something or make something up. Sit back for a second and imagine a break-dancing hippo. If you are right handed, the chance is high that you looked up and to your right. The opposite holds true for lefties.[77]

Ignoring the emotional responses that come from patterns like the above, just because they cannot be articulated, is a mistake. It significantly reduces the advantage you have in face-to-face meetings.

If you have the chance to question management, you should prepare for the meeting by thinking of company-specific questions that challenge them to admit their true motivations and weaknesses. After the meeting, ask yourself if you think you trust them. You can also ask yourself the following questions of management to assess their self-awareness:

- Are they taking credit for things that were not in their control?
- Are they avoiding blame for bad decisions?
- Are they talking very positively about the future and ignoring serious issues in the present?
- Are they too dismissing of legitimate risks in their business?

Of course, most individual investors do not have the opportunity to interview management face-to-face. Nevertheless, there are still many ways to employ social awareness to get an investing edge. It is relatively easy to find interviews of top management on the Internet. Many companies also provide webcasts of recent presentations made at financial conferences on their websites. Finally, you can review conference call transcripts and the chairman's letter in annual reports. When going through all these, ask yourself the questions above to assess what your gut instincts are saying regarding the self-awareness of management. One red flag that usually indicates that a CEO is avoiding blame is when he faults investors for all current company problems. Dick Fuld, the former CEO of bankrupt Lehman Brothers, consistently blamed short sellers for his company's woes. Fuld refused to publicly admit making the mistakes that caused short sellers to get involved in the first place. Another general rule of thumb is that when companies are doing poorly, you want to hear management increasingly talking about the short term. Steve Jobs, who was one of the best visionary CEOs of all time, did this when he took back the CEO job at Apple. Jobs focused on getting the company's cost structure in line and secured a desperately needed investment from Microsoft. As business improved, his communication and focus gradually shifted towards the longer term vision for Apple. When a company misses quarterly expectations, but maintains or even raises longer term growth targets, alarm bells should ring in your head as an investor.

Many former interrogators have written books about to how to spot liars through careful analysis of their statements. None of the yellow flags highlighted below alone tells you anything about trustworthiness, but you should become concerned if you begin to see clusters of these items during a question and answer session with top management.

Yellow flags regarding trustworthiness:

1. Use of qualifiers such as "probably," "sometimes", "fundamentally," "basically," etc. when answering questions. For example, before he was convicted of running a Ponzi scheme, Bernie Madoff said, "In today's regulatory environment, it's *virtually* impossible to violate rules."

2. Not directly answering a "yes" or "no" question, or use of the word "never" instead of "no." This includes avoiding a direct denial when asked about something negative.

3. Use of technical language and buzzwords that avoid answering the question. For example, on RIMM's quarterly conference call in June 2009, Co-CEO Jim Balsillie was asked about why new subscriber growth from business customers was not doing better. Balsillie responded by saying, "I think what is going on with B2B is much more of an architectural shift. I mean that is why MVS is so powerful, in that the new MVS version is about making it a true synchronized PBX, and the SAP stuff is very important, because that is a native services environment. And then all the Wi-Fi for the FMC, and then the BES 5.0 is just getting out..." He went on and on spewing out technical jargon. RIMM's stock declined over 80% in the 2 years following that earnings call.

4. Answers that create distance between the speaker and what he is being questioned about. For example, Bill Clinton described Monica Lewinsky as "that woman" in several interviews.

5. Buying thinking time after questions are asked. This is often done by repeating the question or saying something like "That is a great question!" before answering. Sanjay Kumar, former CEO of Computer Associates would often compliment his questioners during company conference calls before giving his answers. Not only do compliments buy more thinking time, but they also make the questioner less likely to ask tough follow-ups. In 2006, Kumar was sentenced to 12 years in prison for accounting manipulation, securities fraud and lying to investigators.

6. Invocation of a higher power after a tough question is presented. For example, in an interview for a documentary,

Jeffrey Skilling, former CEO of Enron, said, "We are the good guys. We are on the side of angels." In 2006, Skilling was sentenced to 24 years in prison.

7. Use of the present tense for past events. For example, "I walked to the car. A man then *tells* me to give him my wallet." This statement sounds as if the speaker may be fabricating something in real-time as opposed to recalling facts. [78]

8. Incorrect use of articles. In *10 Easy Ways to Spot a Liar*, Mark McClish states, "The indefinite articles "a" and "an" are used to identify someone or something that is unknown. Once the person or thing has been introduced, we are then required to use the definite article 'the.'"[79] McClish, who taught interviewing techniques at the U.S. Marshals Service Training Academy, argues that statements that incorrectly use "the" when the indefinite articles are more appropriate increases the odds that the person answering the question is making up a story. For example, "I saw a man outside my house. The man then pulled out *the* knife." is likely to be untrue.

CHAPTER 10

Developing Social Awareness

"I often studied stocks like I would study people; after a while their reactions to certain circumstances become more predictable." – Jesse Livermore, *Jesse Livermore: World's Greatest Stock Trader*[80]

Like self-awareness, social awareness has been shown to improve with effort. Nevertheless, business schools spend very little time helping students apply social awareness to investing. They primarily teach traditional security analysis. Business schools teach things like how to develop financial forecasts and how to conduct industry analysis. While fundamental security analysis is very important, it is increasingly being commoditized. Thousands of business school graduates, armed with this skill, enter into the investment management industry every year. Moreover, computers are constantly making the analysis easier to do. Financial analysts and business school students should take note that an investment is only attractive when most other potential buyers in the market underestimate its merits. Those who are most socially aware can best judge why others are creating a buying opportunity for you, and what needs to change to influence others to buy after you.

Children develop empathy when they play. A child playing with dolls or toy soldiers often thinks about what each figurine may be feeling. This is the fundamental flaw in the "tiger mother" parenting approach, which devalues playtime. Parents who put no value on play can produce straight-A students. The tradeoff is poor emotional intelligence, which impacts a person's ultimate success and sense of fulfillment. Adults can improve their social awareness in many ways. Like self-analysis, it mainly requires quiet thinking time. As I wrote in Chapter 7, I like to ask myself several questions to develop an investing edge through empathy. I try to put myself in the shoes of a current shareholder and empathize with what she may be feeling given the latest fundamental news and the recent stock price movements. I do the same with someone that may be short the stock and with anyone that may be looking to buy or short the security. With empathy, it is generally easier to *think of what one person is going through* than to think of a large group. This is why charities generally have more fund-raising success when they show you images of a single starving child than when they tell you statistics. When evaluating an investment, it is important to gather as many perspectives as possible. You should talk to people that own the stock, people that are short it and people that follow the company but are neither long nor short. Try to empathize with how each of these people may be feeling and what will make them change their current positioning.

Investors should make it a habit to look at charts once in a while. Instead of getting caught up in esoteric terms such as "ascending triangles" and "head and shoulder patterns," try to think about what the chart is telling you regarding how the current shareholders are feeling. Does it seem like there may be many shareholders who will sell just a little higher when they get back to "break-even?" Does it seem like there may be many people that recently sold the stock, but who would likely buy it back if it retreats slightly? Did the stock just breakout of a range it has been in, even though most market commentators were expecting a possible break down? Remember that technical analysis is mainly a tool for trying to empathize with other shareholders. It is important to keep chart reading simple. You should be cynical about any recommendation from a technician that does not help you to understand what other shareholders may be feeling.

During interviews with management teams of the companies in which you are considering investing, it is important to come prepared and to be observant. It is also vital to be present. Some people may need to remind themselves that they are in the conversation in order to learn, and not to impress the other person. Preparation should involve understanding how people within the organization are incentivized and a review of how management has responded to important questions in the past.

Psychologists offer many other ways to become more socially aware. For example, next time you enter a room full of people, try to assess what the mood in the room is like. Try to figure out who the leader in the group is without someone telling you. Next time you watch a film, try to think about what the characters are feeling. Does the actor do a good job of conveying the appropriate emotions? Next time you sit in a café or on a park bench, do a little "people watching" and try to think about what others may be feeling given their facial expressions. These exercises may sound corny, but researchers have shown them to be highly effective in raising social awareness. Traveling to different places and reading literature have also been shown to improve social awareness. When you put yourself into a foreign environment, you are forced to understand different perspectives. What may seem taboo to you may be quite normal to others. This can compel you to understand how certain things could be possible. To me, travel is much more than sight-seeing and staying in nice resorts. It takes me out of my comfort zone and helps me to understand diverse points of view. Moreover, literature has the power to do the same thing, because it can take you to places that are quite different from your current reality.

Finally, research suggests that the more we interact with empathetic people, the more socially aware we become. You intuitively know which individuals in your social and professional circles are more empathetic than average. Spending more time with these people not only improves your quality of life, but also improves *your* social intelligence. Furthermore, if investment firms would like their employees to be more socially aware, they should make an effort to recruit new employees with this factor in mind. Recruiting will be discussed more towards the end of this book, but it is clear most firms do a horrible job at it given the high level of employee turnover in the investment management industry. Emphasizing emotional intelligence in the recruiting process creates a stronger corporate culture that further strengthens the emotional intelligence of existing employees.

PART 3
INTUITION

CHAPTER 11

What is Intuition?

"The stock market will continue to be essentially what it always was in the past – a place where a big bull market is inevitably followed by a big bear market. In other words, a place where today's free lunches are paid for doubly tomorrow." – Benjamin Graham

In *Blink*, Malcolm Gladwell tells the story of a Cleveland fire lieutenant. The firefighter led his men into a burning house. They turned on the hose and started spraying the fire with water. Suddenly, the fireman thought there was something wrong and ordered his men out. The men vacated the house just in time before the floor they had been standing on collapsed. When asked about how he knew to get out, the fireman could not articulate a rational reason. Something just felt wrong. The firefighter relied upon his intuition.[81] If he had waited to make a decision by analyzing the facts, both the lieutenant and his men would have probably died. Contrary to what many people believe, intuition is not some sort of magical sixth sense. It is an emotion that arises from pattern recognition. The firefighter in Gladwell's story had many years of experience. The expertise, gained from his experience, made his subconscious come to expect certain patterns. Therefore, when he and his men doused water on the fire, he subconsciously had expected the fire to react in a certain way. After the fire did not act in the manner his mind had predicted, his brain generated a negative emotional response. While the fire lieutenant could not explain why he had this "gut" feeling, he was smart enough to act on it and order his men out.

Intuition is a feeling that is generated from pattern recognition. When we build expertise in a field, we are not just accumulating information. Experts develop mental maps so that certain patterns come to be expected. Their expertise becomes so ingrained that they may not understand how or why things seem to make sense. They just do. When events happen that seem consistent with prior patterns, an expert's emotional brain centers generate positive feelings. When something happens that violates the expected pattern, they produce negative emotional responses. For example, Tom Brady, the star NFL quarterback, constantly reviews video footage of his play. He reviews the patterns that led to both positive and negative outcomes. All the hours expended on the field and in review of his play generated a tremendous amount of expertise. The result is that when Brady sees a receiver that is tightly covered by a defender, his brain generates a negative emotional response and he uses his intuition to determine which other receiver to look for. When Brady sees an open receiver, his brain generates a positive feeling. He listens to these gut feelings in determining to whom to pass. In *The Social Animal*, David Brooks states, "The result is that the expert doesn't think more about a subject, she thinks less. She doesn't have to compute the effects of a range of possibilities. Because she has domain expertise, she anticipates how things will fit together."[82]

Like the fire lieutenant in *Blink*, Tom Brady is better off thinking less when on the field. Intuitive choices not only result in speedier decisions, but they also are often better than analytic decisions - at least for people who have built up an adequate amount of expertise. A number of research experiments have shown that when experts ignore intuition, they make worse decisions. Just because intuitions suddenly pop up without active thought does not necessarily make them haphazard thoughts. Gut instincts are valuable products of our expertise. For example, Timothy Wilson at the University of Virginia conducted an experiment in which he showed adults a video of married couples talking to each other. Subjects were asked to predict how long the relationships would last. One group was asked to list their reasoning before making a decision. The second group did not have to offer any rationale. The latter group made much better predictions. When we feel the need to have a rational explanation for every choice we make, we can ignore our intuitions. After all, just like Gladwell's fire lieutenant, we ordinarily cannot adequately articulate why a certain choice feels right or wrong to us.

Virtually all adults have seen enough couples interacting to know what appears healthy. Thus, in Professor Wilson's experiment, almost all the subjects had some sort of expertise about what healthy relationships should look like. Therefore, they could rely on their intuition. Novices, on the other hand, actually do better when they depend more on an analytic framework to make decisions. This is because novices have not yet built up enough necessary expertise. Their gut instincts are less well-informed. Novices use their intellect to decide between many options. Babies learn language and how to walk by carefully selecting each word and thinking about each step. Teenagers learning to drive, actively think about how much pressure to apply to the breaks when going into a sharp turn. Experts intuitively choose a single option and then use their intellect to decide if it is a correct choice. A number of studies have been done on athletes to confirm this. For example, a novice golfer will do better when he thinks about the mechanics of his swing, the distance of the hole and other factors before taking a shot. The more experienced golfer actually does worse when he does so. The experienced golfer is better off thinking less before taking a shot and relying more on intuition.

Professor Wilson's experiment and others like it show how valuable intuition is, and that our gut instincts can easily be ignored when we are forced to be overly analytical in making decisions. This research presents a practical problem for professional investors who need to be taken seriously by their bosses, clients and regulators. How would it sound if your biggest client or the SEC asked you why you owned a particular security in your portfolio and you simply said that it "felt right" to buy it? While money managers have always needed to have analytic justifications of their investment decisions, this pressure has increased with more government scrutiny and demands from clients for transparency. The result is relatively low use of intuitive decision-making. In the 1980s, Peter Lynch made a decision to evaluate a potential investment in Dunkin Donuts. He did so largely because he liked the company's donuts, and because he had an intuitive feeling that others would also like them. He started his investment process harnessing his gut instinct and followed it up with rational analysis in a way that did not suppress his initial intuition. Today, there are relatively few investors that operate the same way Peter Lynch did then. The increased use of screening tools and the ascent of quantitative funds have suppressed the role of an expert's intuition in idea selection in the overall market. This has created a great opportunity.

In this book, I try to demystify the concept of intuition with respect to investing. Instead of something like ESP or a God-given gift, I affirm that gut instinct comes from pattern recognition. The reason why intuition seems mysterious is because gut feelings can occur instantaneously and without conscious thought. Nevertheless, intuition is difficult to acquire and use safely. If we followed every gut feeling, we would get ourselves into a lot of trouble. In the next chapter, I offer a process for utilizing our gut instincts in a safe way. Optimal decision-making should start with the harnessing of intuition, but should be safeguarded with logic. We can and should still have analytic justifications for our investment choices. However, assuming we have built up enough expertise, our decisions should start with intuition. In Chapter 13, I illustrate how intuition can best be developed. Gut instincts come from experience, but experience does not necessarily lead to expertise and useful intuitions. I offer a process for attaining the most out of our experiences. Intuition should be used for finding new investment opportunities. It should also be utilized for sensing danger with existing investments and for portfolio construction. Finally, I show some ways we can leverage the intuition of others to make better decisions.

While I reference many prominent psychologists in this book, I disagree with many of them when it comes to intuition and investing. They argue that the stock market is too complex and random for intuition to be developed and utilized. I find this amazing since many of the same psychologists seem to think that intuition can, and should, be utilized by soldiers in war as well as by CEOs. War is arguably at least as random and complex as the stock market. After all, you could even be killed by your own comrades! Furthermore, a CEO's decisions are largely about investing. Deciding on whether or not to build a new factory, or to conduct research for a new product, or to hire a new CFO are all decisions about how best to invest time and money. Some psychologists also cite the fact that a large percentage of mutual funds underperform market indices every year. To them, this is proof that intuition built from investing experience does not translate into better decision-making. While it is true that most mutual funds underperform, a small percentage outperform consistently, which suggests to me that there is a handful of investors that have a "secret sauce." Moreover, the fact that many of the statistically best investors seem to come from places where they had similar training (i.e., disciples of Benjamin Graham or Julian Robertson) implies that the "secret sauce" can be learned.

Of the hundreds of investment ideas I heard pitched by analysts every year, very few struck a chord immediately. I knew these were great trades even before the analysts finished a few sentences and before I dissected the financials and specific company and industry dynamics myself. Why did I gravitate towards certain investment ideas and not others? Just like any other expert, professional investors have the capacity to build intuition through understanding patterns. The longer term investor builds expertise that provides gut instincts regarding the business cycle, competency of management, a company's sustainable competitive advantages, regulatory risks, and technology risks as well as many other factors that can impact a company's earnings power, growth rate and market valuation over the long term. While the stock market as a whole can seem very complex and somewhat random, there are many patterns that recur with high regularity. Some investors have made a living primarily focusing on a certain type of pattern. For example, Ray Dalio of Bridgewater, one of the largest and most successful hedge funds, affirms that business cycles follow a repetitious pattern. He also believes that these business cycles occur within much longer term debt cycles.[83] He relies upon his intuition and analysis to determine where the economy is currently operating within these cycles to determine which asset classes are best to be involved in. David Einhorn of Greenlight Capital seems to have an intuitive feel for investing in companies that have recently been spun out of larger organizations. Greenlight appears to have made a meaningful share of its historical profits from investments in these types of companies. The firm is very good at recognizing which spin-offs will produce outsized returns for investors. This involves having gut instincts regarding which companies will benefit most from independence and increased management attention as well as intuition as to the competency of management. Many of the Tiger cubs – hedge funds founded by former partners and employees of Julian Robertson's Tiger Management – seem to have an intuitive feel for investing in underappreciated growth companies. They regularly

144

recognize when a secular trend can be more powerful than most others expect. All these great investors have intuitions that help them to cut through uncertainty in certain situations. What seems unpredictable to most market participants is somewhat familiar. Therefore, these master investors can take on risk when others are more fearful. They profit as uncertainty declines.

As an investor that primarily focuses on the technology sector, I have also noticed many fundamental patterns that tend to recur. For example, recall from Chapter 7 that I shorted shares of Research in Motion. The initial thought of deciding to work on RIMM as a potential short came from recognizing a pattern that I have seen many times before: successful technology companies often find it difficult to make revolutionary changes. This makes them very susceptible whenever a revolutionary change does occur in their niche. Professor Clayton Christensen of Harvard Business School describes this as "the innovator's dilemma." For example, when RIMM was the leading smartphone company, it had many customers that liked its physical QWERTY keyboard. Its customers primarily used its products for mobile email. If RIMM diverted its research and development focus towards products that did not have physical keyboards, it risked damaging many of its existing customer relationships. As a result, RIMM's research effort mainly concerned incremental improvements. After Apple introduced the iPhone, it was clear that RIMM's dominant market share would be at risk. By the way, I do not think that Apple is immune to the innovator's dilemma. Note that similar to the way RIMM did, Apple now only makes incremental changes to the iPhone. The latest version of the iPhone appears relatively similar to the very first version. If Apple were to make a revolutionary change, it would risk alienating its app developer community. Apple only makes incremental changes to its iPhone, because the company wants older applications to work on any new phones it sells. Therefore, like RIMM was, Apple is now susceptible to a revolutionary change in the smartphone industry. Until such a change happens, Apple will probably continue to do well. It is possible that a radical change never happens again in this industry. However, if and whenever a revolutionary shift does happen, my gut will likely tell me to be negatively biased towards Apple in the same way I had a negative gut feeling towards RIMM.

Helpful gut instincts can also be developed regarding entire industries. In Chapter 13, I will provide an example of a "pattern" for the semiconductor industry. Moreover, gut feelings can be thematic. For example, you could have the intuition that smart phones will cannibalize older generation phones much faster than expected. This can lead to both long and short investments into several different industries and companies. A gut feeling that high dividend stocks with large market capitalizations will outperform is another example of a thematic intuition. Category-wide gut instincts like these are usually more helpful than stock specific ones. First, they generate more investments ideas to evaluate. Second, getting a theme correct increasingly matters much more than being right about the business prospects of a specific company. According to Adam Parker, US equity strategist at Morgan Stanley, the impact of macro-economic factors on a typical stock's annual return has increased by about 60% in the last 6 years to account for over half of a stock's performance.[84] Some of this increase is probably cyclical, but I think most of it is structural. For example, 10 years ago I didn't need to have a view on Brazil when I decided about an investment in Intel. There weren't many computers being sold to Brazilians. Now, Brazil is a more important end market. Furthermore, the world has become more interconnected with ever more globally coordinated policy decisions. What happens in Brazil can easily impact computer demand in many other countries. Therefore, since the world is only becoming more interconnected, thematic intuitions and gut feelings regarding macro-economic variables will continue to be even more important than they were in the past.

When compared to a long term investor, a short term trader's intuition is very different. A good trader can take advantage of the common mistakes others make. As discussed in Chapter 3, people make common investing errors caused by their emotional biases. Because these mistakes are made relatively frequently by other participants in the market, a smart and experienced trader can spot them within an overall stock market that appears random to most outside observers. A good trader also tries to build intuition that anticipates the intuitions of other participants in the market. For example, many traders and investors have recognized a pattern regarding when a stock breaks out to make a new all-time high. A breakout often leads to a flurry of buying activity – some of this buying activity comes from quantitative funds that have trading algorithms, which are triggered whenever a stock makes a new high. A smart short term trader can potentially take advantage of this "intuition" of the masses by buying just ahead of the breakout. A trader's intuition involves understanding the personalities of the current holders and short sellers of a particular security and understanding what will make them make certain decisions. This is a difficult skill to learn and because the market's participants are constantly trying to be one step ahead of each other, it is very difficult to be a consistently good trader. Success can lead to complacency, which can result in one becoming a "has-been" that some other star traders will outperform.

The longer term investor's intuition can also become obsolete over time. For example, others will eventually develop the expertise that Einhorn and his team have developed regarding spin offs. These new experts will bid up the initial price of promising investments at the time of the spin off to largely anticipate most of the fundamental improvements of the business. This will result in reduced opportunity for Einhorn unless his firm adapts and develops new intuitions. Therefore, the most successful investment firms over the long term are those that are open to change. Warren Buffett's investing approach has evolved tremendously during his long career. In the beginning of his career, he strictly followed the value approach of Benjamin Graham. However, later in his career, he actually developed into more of a growth investor. For example, while he historically shunned investments in the technology sector, he recently made a relatively large investment in IBM in 2011.

If you are evaluating an investment into a money management fund, you should first recognize what type of investor you are dealing with. If a shorter term trader has not been performing well recently, it can be a sign that she has not kept up with being anticipatory of the market. On the other hand, an investor that has a longer time horizon should not be judged based on short term results. Over the long term, the firms that are most open to change and that focus on building new intuitions will be most successful.

We live in a world where quantitative financial analysts use powerful computers to recognize patterns in the market. Quant funds have taken away some of the profit from traders by doing some of what traders historically did in a much more efficient way. Moreover, these quant funds are increasingly competing with each other. The competitive advantage humans have over computers is the ability to develop intuitions on factors that are not quantifiable. For example, computers did not appreciate how groundbreaking Apple's iPhone was in the smartphone industry. Computers do not have the ability to recognize if a new manager has the competencies required for a particular business to succeed. Computers do not recognize how much less competitive certain industries can become after consolidation occurs. Computers do not understand how sustainable a certain secular growth trend can be. The list of examples goes on and on. There is no limit to the gut instincts we can develop to have an investing edge. In the next couple of chapters, I address how we can safeguard our intuitions and how we can best develop them.

CHAPTER 12

Using Intuition Safely

"That a company makes a popular product doesn't mean you should automatically buy the stock. There is a lot more you have to know before you invest." – Peter Lynch, *Learn to Earn*[85]

If we just invest based on what "feels right" we risk falling victim to one of the biases discussed in Chapter 3. Nevertheless, the best traders and investors seem to use something more than rational analysis. Even those who have a highly analytical process for evaluating investments often rely on their intuition to decide on which potential investments to analyze. They also rely on their intuition to make subjective opinions regarding management competency, a new product's potential, regulatory risks, competitive dynamics and many other factors that can impact a potential investment. Therefore, intuition can be both dangerous and very helpful. In this chapter, I discuss a process we can use to derive the most out of our gut feelings without having them negatively impact us.

Let's consider how chess grandmasters decide their moves. According to Garry Kasparov, former World Chess Champion, "The total number of positions in a game of chess is greater than the number of atoms in the universe."[86] Given this, it is impossible for a chess player to evaluate alternative moves in an entirely rational manner. Kasparov also does not believe that high intelligence necessarily makes someone a great chess player. He writes, "Elite players don't in fact look ahead that much further than considerably weaker players while solving chess problems. They can, on occasion, but it doesn't define their superior play."[87] The best chess players rely on their gut instincts and usually formulate their moves within 3 seconds after their opponents complete their turns. These moves feel right to them based on how the pieces are currently laid out on the board and how they would like the board to eventually look. This intuition is not magic. Rather, it is the result of years of study and practice. While they listen to their gut, they also know that it should not be overly relied upon. Grandmasters may intuitively come up with great moves very quickly, but they also spend the majority of their playing time making sure the move is safe. If their reasoning indicates that the move is overly risky, the grandmasters rely upon their intuition to quickly come up with another move to evaluate.

Like chess grandmasters, investors who have built adequate expertise should employ gut instincts. Not doing so would ignore years of experience and training. However, these intuitions should be safeguarded with logic. In *The Power of Intuition*, Gary Klein states, "We don't want to rely entirely on impulses. Impulses and intuition have to be balanced with deliberate, rational analysis. But rational analysis can never substitute for intuition." After reading work from psychologists like Gary Klein and reflecting on my own experiences as an investor, I have developed a process that helps me to safeguard my gut feelings:

Step 1: Remember that intuition is only valuable if it concerns something in which you have ample experience.

The first question to ask yourself when you are experiencing a gut feeling regarding a particular investment decision is whether you are actually employing your expertise. If not, then you should be very hesitant to rely on your emotions. For example, an individual who has spent her entire career as a short term trader of highly liquid securities should be very hesitant to follow her gut instincts on an illiquid investment that has a very long term payoff. Similarly, an investor who has spent most of his career following the retail sector should be hesitant to invest in a biotech company. The competencies required to make a good investment decision in retail are very different than those required in biotech. The two sectors have very few common patterns that lead to investing success. This seems like a very basic step, but it is surprising how many big mistakes can be avoided through its use. Many of the highest profile investing errors occur because success leads to overconfidence in investing outside of one's core competency.

Step 2: Remind yourself of your emotional biases.

When one has a positive gut feeling regarding a possible investment decision, it is often not clear whether the feeling is actually intuition. There is always the chance that such a feeling is a result of an emotional bias that is harmful to investing. The best defense against these biases is self-awareness. We need to constantly remind ourselves of our specific vulnerabilities. When we make good decisions, we should reflect not only on the fact sets we had at the time of the decisions, but also about how we felt when we made the decisions. Similarly, we should try to remember how we felt when we made poor decisions. Many of the best investors are self-aware enough to know whether their feelings are potentially harmful or helpful. This state of self-awareness is very difficult to achieve and I still have a long way to go, myself. However, I believe that just by keeping a journal of my trading activities I have come a long way towards identifying my feelings. This has not only helped me avoid many mistakes, but I think it has also helped in generating positive investment decisions. We should also try to do our best to make our intuitions more explicit so that they can be analyzed rationally. This is the purpose of Steps 3 to 5.

Step 3: Ask yourself whether the investment reminds you of a previous situation.

Our intuitions are based on pattern recognition. Therefore, we should try to take the time to link our gut instincts to these patterns. A fireman or a soldier in the middle of action does not usually have the time to do this step, but an investor does. We can think of a previous situation that is similar to the fact set at hand. If we cannot remember any other prior investment that seems similar, we should be hesitant to rely on our gut feelings. Very few investment decisions will match up to prior choices perfectly, but we should take note of the similarities and the differences as best as we can.

Step 4: Know the security and understand your risk / reward.

While there is no substitute for good intuition to determine which investment ideas merit further investigation, there is also no substitute for doing the fundamental research to understand specific industry and company dynamics. I do not spend much time in this book on security analysis. It's not because I do not think it is important. It is because there is already a plethora of books out there concerning security analysis. Developing an understanding of what you could possibly make on an investment if things go right and what you could lose if risk factors materialize is a basic aspect of investing. One needs to also try to estimate probabilities of certain positive and negative events occurring. When unanticipated events occur, one should know the investment well enough to quickly recalibrate its risk and reward potential. All this can only be done if one has a solid understanding of how a given business and industry operate.

Step 5: Bounce ideas off someone else.

Psychologists have shown how others can spot whether you have biases better than you can. Daniel Kahneman states, "Questioning your intuitions is unpleasant when you face the stress of a big decision. More doubt is the last thing you want when you are in trouble. The upshot is that it is much easier to identify a minefield when you observe others wandering into it than when you are about to do so."[88] Therefore, talking to others about how a current decision reminds you of a successful investment in the past can be helpful. If others are aware of your most common emotional biases, they can help determine whether your feeling is actually helpful intuition or not. Most portfolio managers ask their analysts to summarize the highlights of the bull case and list the risk factors for a potential investment. This summary is not enough and only going this far can put too much emphasis on certain factors that can be more easily quantified and articulated. In order to get the most out of intuition and receive the most feedback, it is better to start your description with a prior situation that resembles the current choice. Your partner can help flesh out how the current decision may be similar to or different from prior choices you have made. The point of this step is to better understand if you can trust your intuition, and that happens when you try to make sense of what former pattern is responsible for producing the gut feeling.

Step 6: Maintain freedom to change your mind, and set up trip wires.

After going through steps 1-5, you should have a reasonable amount of trust in your intuition. However, you will be more comfortable utilizing gut feelings if you remain open to changing your mind. George Soros often relies on his gut instincts in making investment decisions. While his intuition is excellent, especially with respect to macroeconomic cycles, his best strength appears to be his flexibility. He is constantly on the lookout for flaws in his thesis and he is very comfortable reversing his position if he thinks he is wrong. Stanley Druckenmiller, who worked for Soros for many years, also has this strength. For example, just before the 1987 stock market crash, Druckenmiller had significant long exposure to the market. He realized he was wrong, and quickly reversed his position in the morning of Black Monday. He wound up having a relatively good year despite being incorrectly positioned going into the crash. One way to maintain flexibility is to set up trip wires. In an investing context, trip wires are events that should not occur if your thesis and intuition is right. For example, let's assume you invest in a company partially because you believe that management is highly competent. A trip wire for this investment could be poor execution by management on a new product release. Another trip wire could be the company overpaying for an acquisition that does not seem to make sense to you. Trip wires are discussed in more detail in Chapter 14 when the intuition that helps sense danger is addressed.

I describe the steps above as a "process" but if followed enough times, it becomes very natural. For example, when someone pitches me an investment in a sector in which I have no experience, I automatically know to proceed cautiously. I have identified certain patterns that tend to recur over and over again and I try to stick with investments that fit those patterns. Whenever I have a gut feeling regarding a specific investment, I almost habitually try to remind myself of a similar prior fact set. If the potential investment does not remind me of any pattern I have seen successfully work before, I pass on the investment and move on. If after understanding the company's fundamentals, I cannot come up with risk / reward characteristics that make sense, I move on. If after talking to another investor, it becomes apparent that there are too many major differences between the current situation and the pattern I thought the investment fit into, I move on. This is a somewhat similar process to how a chess grandmaster may dismiss his initial gut feeling. After careful analysis, he realizes that his initial gut feeling is not safe. However, the chess grandmaster still utilizes his intuition to come up with another possible move to evaluate. He follows this process over and over again until he comes up with a move that he intuitively feels good about and appears logically acceptable. Like the best investors, great chess players are those who have built up enough pattern recognition / expertise / intuition to point them in the direction of the best possible moves. They make sure the game is played so that their competencies are best utilized. They also have a good analytical process for making sure their gut instincts are safe. Finally, they maintain mental flexibility. Great chess players may decide to retreat from an attack or realize that they are being overly defensive. Similarly, great investors often reverse their positions after they realize they are wrong or after their trip wires are triggered.

Here are two concrete examples of how intuition should be balanced with reasoning. In the first example, I describe how a gut feeling to invest in Veeco Instruments (VECO) was safeguarded by fundamental analysis. I also briefly show how I gained an empathetic edge with VECO. The analysis combined with my intuition and empathetic feelings led to increased conviction. In the second example, I show how I realized my gut feelings regarding an investment into the flat panel component industry were incorrect. I used logic to override my intuition, and successfully missed out on making a very bad investment.

Example 1 – Using Intuition Safely

In the beginning of 2012, my intuition led me to evaluate VECO as an investment. Veeco Instruments is a manufacturer of process equipment technology. It has leading market share in equipment used to make Light Emitting Diodes (LEDs), and is the leader in process equipment for making hard disk drives. It also has a relatively small business exposed to solar panels. In Q4 2011, LED's represented 78% of sales, data storage represented 17% and solar was 5%. Similar to most capital equipment businesses, the company's earnings are highly cyclical. The LED industry was suffering from industry oversupply. As a result, VECO's stock and earnings were down significantly over the last year. Over 20% of the total shares outstanding were actually sold short. When the company reported its results for Q4 2011, its guidance for 2012 was significantly lower than Wall Street's projections. Nevertheless, despite the big cut to expectations, VECO's stock actually closed *up* on the day following the announcement. VECO reminded me of other highly cyclical technology stocks that tend to bottom out when they no longer go down after reporting bad news. While the potential investment seemed to fit a pattern that I had seen work before, I still safeguarded my gut instincts by going through the process described above. I had ample experience investing in cyclical technology companies, so I felt that my expertise was relevant for a decision with VECO. I reminded myself of my emotional biases and asked myself which specific investments in the past seemed most similar to VECO. As I learned more about VECO's business and the LED industry, I realized that the risk-to-reward was quite attractive. The risk was limited since the company's large net cash position had been close to 50% of its market capitalization. Furthermore, the company was still earning money despite the terrible industry conditions. I also realized that because company guidance was lowered so significantly, the company would be now much more likely to meet or even exceed estimates going forward. VECO's management was guiding for its business to continue to get worse when there were already several industry data-points that suggested stabilization. For example, some of the Taiwanese LED chip companies, which were customers of VECO, were publicly talking about how their utilization rates were rising. Once their utilization rates get to a high enough level, these customers usually start to make orders for more capital equipment. It seemed only a matter of time until this would happen. At the same time, the reward was significant since LEDs were expected to replace the very large incandescent bulb market longer term. Several countries had actually already enacted regulations that would phase out energy inefficient incandescent bulbs. If the company could eventually get earnings back somewhere close to prior peak levels, the upside on the stock would be very significant. I talked about the idea with a couple of friends who also have experience investing in cyclical companies. They helped me to think of additional risks so that I could set up trip wires for the investment. For example, VECO had about 50% market share and had been gaining share. Applied Materials recently entered the market as a new competitor and as of the beginning of 2012 did not have much traction with customers. Therefore, a risk factor for the investment would be excessive price competition and lost market share to Applied Materials. I set up a trip wire to reduce the position if I saw this occurring.

I also developed an empathetic edge for the investment. I knew the short sellers had thought consensus estimates were too high. However, after the company guided down significantly, their reasoning for being short was no longer valid. They would look to quickly lock-in their gains if the company actually started making or beating estimates as my analysis suggested. Furthermore, most people who still owned the stock had held on as the company's business prospects deteriorated significantly. If they did not capitulate by now, only another significant drop in the stock would lead them to sell. Given the large net cash position and my reasoning that earnings appeared achievable, if not beatable, I thought this scenario unlikely. Moreover, VECO's shareholders probably felt encouraged by the improving utilization rates of the company's customers in Asia. As long as their utilization rates did not decline, the company's shareholders would remain hopeful of an industry turnaround. Finally, VECO aggressively bought its own shares in 2011 about 10% below where it was trading at the beginning of

2012. This gave me additional comfort. The company's board of directors possibly developed a positive association bias from buying at this price. They experienced a positive outcome. If the stock dipped back down to that same price, I reasoned that there was some chance the company would step in to support its shares again.

My initial intuition combined with my fundamental analysis and my empathetic realizations resulted in my relatively high conviction in the investment. In the first half of 2012, VECO was my largest new investment as well as my biggest winner. The stock significantly outperformed the market after reporting Q1 2012 results in early May that beat expectations.

Figure 13

Example 2 – Safeguarding Intuition:

In the fall of 2011, my intuition suggested that I evaluate the flat panel companies like AU Optronics (AUO) and LG Display (LPL). These companies make the liquid crystal displays (LCDs) that are found in TVs, computer monitors, tablet computers, cell phones, etc. The LCD or "flat panel" is usually the most expensive component of a TV and the TV market represents the majority of the flat panel market. TV set makers, like Sony, are important customers of AUO and LPL. The industry has historically been very cyclical and has followed a pattern that I had seen repeated several times. When the panel makers like AU Optronics had insufficient supply to meet demand, they would be able to raise prices. This would improve earnings and also lift their stock prices. The panel makers would then increase capital expenditures to grow supply. This involved building new factories, which took some time. Because the TV set makers had increased costs as a result of the higher flat panel component pricing, they were sometimes forced to raise the pricing of TVs. This caused end demand for TVs to weaken about at the same time when new flat panel supply came online. This eventually led to industry oversupply of flat panels, which resulted in weaker margins for the panel makers and lower stock prices. This oversupply would last until retail TV prices declined enough to stimulate increased demand and for the cycle to repeat. By the fall of 2011, I had seen this cycle repeat many times. It seemed like everything was in place for the pattern to repeat yet again. The flat panel industry was in oversupply. This caused the margins and the stock prices for companies like AUO to decline. Sony and other TV set makers passed on most of the lower component cost pricing to consumers. My gut instinct told me that if the prior pattern would hold, it would only be a matter of time until the lower retail TV pricing would stimulate increased demand; thereby, ending the down-cycle for the flat panel companies. Nevertheless, this was a situation where safeguarding my intuition with logic prevented me from making a mistake. When I rationally evaluated what was different this time around, I realized that household penetration of LCD TVs had climbed significantly over the years. Since many people already had multiple LCD TVs, they would no longer feel compelled to buy additional TVs even if prices declined significantly. Logic told me that there was something wrong with my intuition. Even though retail TV prices continued to be weak, 2011 Holiday sales remained depressed.

Please note that the drivers of intuition are very difficult to articulate. I try to provide you with some examples of "patterns" that produce gut feelings. I oversimplify. In reality, intuition comes about from a confluence of factors – many of which I cannot describe. For example, there was much more that contributed to my initial instinct to evaluate VECO as an investment. These causes ranged from anecdotal evidence of stabilizing industry conditions to seeing how other cyclical stocks were performing. It is *not* necessary to fully comprehend the root causes of your intuitive feelings. Assuming you have built up the necessary expertise, what is more important is to make sure you harness your gut instincts despite their nebulous nature.

CHAPTER 13

Developing Intuition

"We both insist on a lot of time being available almost every day to just sit and think. That is very uncommon in American business." – Charlie Munger

In *Outliers,* Malcolm Gladwell asserts that 10,000 hours of practice is a prerequisite for expertise.[89] Nevertheless, I know many people with well over 10,000 hours of investing experience that do not appear to be experts. While experience is necessary, it does not necessarily lead to helpful intuition. This chapter addresses how we can get the most out of our experiences so as to develop useful gut instincts.

Let's continue with the chess analogy. The best chess players spend more time reviewing their play and the play of others than actually playing. When they lose a game, they try to figure out what they did wrong. When they win, they focus on what they did right. Superior chess grandmasters are self-aware enough to know what aspect of their game they need to improve. If they tend to be weak in the beginning of the game, they spend more time studying opening moves. If they are inclined to make poor moves at the end of the game, they conduct drills where they review older matches when an excellent player overcame a disadvantage and surprisingly won. They try to see if they can emulate that great player. The writer Geoff Colvin describes this process as "deliberate practice." In *How Life Imitates Chess,* Garry Kasparov states, "Too often we just live with the results and move on, repeating the same flawed process with the same flawed results."[90] Kasparov believes that the secret to success in chess and in most other endeavors is a relentless review of prior decisions and focused practice on areas that require improvement. Critiquing prior decisions develops intuition, because it increases the odds that prior patterns stick somewhere in one's mind. The result is that next time a similar problem is presented, the good chess player either has higher confidence in making the correct move again or has improved his intuition so that it points him towards the better move.

Investors should build expertise in a similar fashion. Trading coach Ari Kiev states, "Just like coaches often review game films to find out what needs to be tweaked before the next big game, traders must learn to look back on their decisions to see what could have been changed that might have created a more favorable outcome."[91] This requires hard work and a shift in attitude. I had the good fortune to have Michael Karsch of Karsch Capital Management as my mentor for eight years. Michael is known in the hedge fund industry as a "difficult" portfolio manager to work for. This is because he places very high emphasis on reviewing prior decisions, especially the bad ones. After reflecting and writing this book, I have come to appreciate his effort. By forcing me to constantly think about what I could have done better, Michael helped me build expertise. Moreover, he instilled in me a drive to constantly review my decisions without anyone's coaching. In an industry with relatively high employee turnover, there are very few hedge fund managers who put in that much investment into their analysts. It is much easier to just fire analysts who make bad decisions, rather than to help them understand what they could have done better. He is a "difficult" person to work for because he expects more than just financial analysis and stock picking. He expects his analysts to adhere to a corporate culture that involves introspection, flexibility of mind and humility. When I first started at Karsch Capital, it was a tough adjustment. I had always done well in school and in prior jobs and activities. I was not used to being criticized. I was ashamed of making mistakes and was defensive. Over time, I came to understand the culture and as I built stronger intuitions, my performance improved. Every bad and good decision became an opportunity to learn something about myself and about stock picking. Moreover, because I became increasingly self-critical of my decisions, Michael actually became "easier" to work for. It was great to have a mentor that encouraged me to develop a personal philosophy around "deliberate practice." However, a mentor is not needed. In the end, it is a personal decision.

After reviewing the fact set around prior investment decisions, investors tend to see patterns within the overall market that can lead to success. Recognizing these patterns is an investor's competitive advantage. I do not want to give away too many of the patterns I personally look for, but just to give an example, let's consider what I like to see before making an investment in the semiconductor industry. The semiconductor industry is highly cyclical. This is in part driven by inventory cycles. The semiconductor companies (e.g. Intel) sell to the electronics manufacturers (e.g. HP), who then ship their product to retailers (e.g. Best Buy) and distributors. When end demand for computers and other electronic goods is very strong, the retailers and distributors of these products build up extra buffer inventory to meet the rising demand. The manufacturers of the electronic goods also build up extra buffer stock of finished goods as well as of their raw materials. Therefore, when end demand is strong, the semiconductor companies are usually selling more units than are being consumed by end demand. The difference is being built up as inventory in the supply chain. This makes the chip manufacturers very susceptible to any weakness in end demand. Whenever end demand weakens, the electronics manufacturers and retailers decide to reduce their buffer stock inventories. This causes the revenues of semiconductor companies to drop significantly until the excess inventory in the channel is worked through. Any investor in the semiconductor industry is aware of cyclicality caused by inventory swings. However, it takes a certain degree of expertise to know when is the best time to take advantage of the cyclicality as an investor. If one waits until business at semiconductor companies rebounds, one is often too late. When a certain fact set becomes apparent, my gut recognizes a pattern and tells me that it is the right time to evaluate buying semiconductor stocks. For example, if the industry is in a downturn, a fact set that would get me excited involves: (i) some confirmation from retailers like Best Buy or manufacturers like Dell that end demand is stabilizing or even starting to improve; (ii) significant inventory taken out of the supply chain; (iii) increased merger activity in which larger semiconductor companies are buying smaller ones for cash; (iv) increased insider buying, especially from insiders with a good track record with their purchases; (v) significantly reduced capital expenditure by semiconductor companies, which should lead to very low supply growth over the next couple of years; (vi) high pessimism from other market participants indicated by high and rising short interest in semiconductor stocks and poor relative ratings by sell-side brokerage firms; and (vii) semiconductor stocks not reacting too negatively to bad news such as missing quarterly earnings expectations. The stock reactions allow me to empathize with the current holders of the stock. When a stock goes up on bad news or does not go down much, it tells me that there are many shareholders that were already expecting weak results. Therefore, any improvement in business is likely to be a positive surprise and to be good for the stock price. The seven points outlined above are just a handful of items that would constitute the "pattern" that would spark my gut instinct with respect to making an investment in the semiconductor industry. They may seem unrealistic to expect all at once, but I have noticed all these factors exist at the same time at least once every 3-5 years in the semiconductor industry. Most recently, this "pattern" became apparent in the fall of 2011 and preceded strong gains for most chip stocks.

There are a couple of important characteristics that are unique to investing. This is where the chess analogy breaks down. First, randomness plays a much larger role with investing. Second, investing intuitions become obsolete over time. It is because of these differences that very few investors appear to have good intuition over the long term. Below, I expand on these unique features of investing and discuss how intuition can be built despite them:

Problem 1: Randomness plays a much larger role with investing.

There are many factors that can generate a positive outcome for an investment decision and some of these variables can be quite accidental. For example, suppose Martha decided to invest in an oil company because there was a change in management. Martha believed prior management was running the business very inefficiently. For example, the company had two private jets when similar size oil companies had none. Her intuition told her that new management will be much more competent and shareholder friendly. This pattern reminded Martha of similar inefficiently run companies that turned out to be good investments after a management change. She did not have a strong view on where oil prices would go in the short or long term. If, after making the investment, an unexpected war in the Persian Gulf caused oil prices and stock prices of all oil companies to spike significantly, how should Martha review her decision? On the one hand, her decision led to a positive outcome. On the other hand, randomness was the key driver of her making money. Most investors in Martha's shoes will think that they made a good decision, because they made money even though a random event could have also caused oil prices to drop significantly. They do not realize that they were lucky. People have a tendency to minimize the role of good luck in their decision-making and overestimate the role of bad luck. Therefore, most investors actually learn nothing from many of their experiences, or even take away the wrong lessons. Because they associate a positive bias towards investments like this, they might be inclined to bet even bigger when the next one comes along that seems similar. Inevitably, luck doesn't go their way and they lose money.

Solution to Randomness

It is important to remember that expertise is developed through the *review of the decision-making process rather than outcomes.* When evaluating an investment decision, it is important to try to take into account random variables. In this case, even though Martha made money and relied on her intuition, there was a flaw in her process. She made a bet on an investment that is highly sensitive to commodity price fluctuations without having any view on the commodity. If she really wanted to follow her intuition and analysis, she should have hedged out the exposure to oil price changes – for example, she could have shorted another stock highly sensitive to oil. Martha could have also just decided to not invest. She could have realized that while this pattern may have worked with other industries, the randomness in oil price fluctuations had the potential to overwhelm any efficiency improvements new management could make. This is why I began this book discussing self-awareness. Only someone self-aware will admit when luck bails them out of making a bad decision. It is important to focus on patterns that seem to occur over and over again within the overall market. Investors and traders should also try to focus their decision-making around patterns that have relatively low chances of being significantly impacted by random events. They should attempt to hedge out their exposure to some random events, if possible. Randomness can never be completely eliminated when investing. However, what is most important is that one is honest with oneself with respect to the role of luck. Only then can one actually learn from a prior decision.

Problem 2: Investing intuitions become obsolete.

Let's assume that Martha's gut instinct was actually helpful. She identified a pattern that tends to occur over and over again in the overall market. The pattern is that very poorly managed companies in growing industries tend to outperform after the CEO is replaced by someone who is much more competent and shareholder friendly. She also relies on her intuition to determine how good the new management will be. Of course, random events will imply that not every poorly managed company with a positive management change will outperform. However, after reviewing many of her prior decisions that fit a similar fact set and after being honest with herself about the role of randomness, she believes that she has built considerable expertise with investing in companies that fit this specific pattern. Martha becomes rich over several years by employing her intuition with respect to this pattern. Eventually other investors will catch on. They will either recognize the pattern the same way Martha did or they will try to understand how Martha is making so much money and will emulate her. Eventually, Martha's intuition will become obsolete. Previously, not many people took notice of management transitions and Martha would acquire stock at almost the same price as where it was trading prior to the management change announcement. Now, stocks that Martha wants to buy spike up immediately after the management change announcement. They go up so much that the risk / reward of the investment is no longer practical. As a result, Martha has a much tougher time making money even though she has much more investing experience now than she did several years ago.

Solution to Obsolescence

One needs to remember that every pattern in the market has the potential to become obsolete. Some quantitative trading algorithms that seem to make money become obsolete in a few days, while other patterns employed by longer term investors can make money for several decades. Obsolescence is another reason why intuition needs to be safeguarded with logic. If Martha does not go through the effort of analytically understanding her risk / reward, she will inevitably make poor investment choices. The only solution to obsolescence is constant evolution. The best firms are those that foster a culture of intuition building. They maintain flexibility to change their approach to where new opportunities lie. Investors like Martha should not become complacent with a certain expertise. They need to try to constantly build new intuitions.

While reviewing your prior decisions is probably the best technique to build intuition, it is not the only way. Chess players often review the moves of prior great players. They see how the pieces were laid out on the board just before a great player made an excellent move. They try to put themselves in the other player's shoes and understand how he made that great decision. By doing so, they are actually building intuition from the experience of someone else. Eddie Lampert of ESL Investments seems to have done something similar. Soon after graduating college, Lampert said he studied Warren Buffett's investment decisions. For example, according to a 2004 cover story in Bloomberg BusinessWeek, "Lampert went back and read GEICO's annual reports in the couple of years preceding Buffett's initial investment in the 1970's."[92] While studying the investment decisions of great investors is certainly helpful, one can also build intuition by studying the bad and good decisions of colleagues. Good organizations are structured in such a way that prior decisions are objectively reviewed not only by the people that made the decision, but also by others in the organization. This allows for everyone to learn and build intuition from not only their prior decisions, but also from the decisions of others in the organization. Visualization exercises are another way to develop intuition. When an investor imagines an investment failing and tries to visualize all the possible reasons for the loss, he develops intuition as to what negative developments to look out for. Visualizing a range of scenarios for variables outside of one's control can also aid an investor in making decisions for position sizing and portfolio construction. The gut feelings for sensing danger and portfolio construction will be addressed in more detail in the next chapter.

The bad news is that building helpful gut instincts is hard work. It requires constantly reviewing one's decision-making process in an objective manner. This entails high self-awareness to filter through random events that can impact outcomes. Intuition can also be built through reviewing decisions of others. This requires empathy. Finally, even after expertise is created, a good investor needs to prepare for its eventual obsolescence. You need to have flexibility of mind to develop intuition in new possible patterns. The good news is that once truly helpful intuition is built, you will be among a select group of investors with competitive advantage.

CHAPTER 14

Sensing Danger, Portfolio Construction, and Leveraging the Intuition of Others

"I was sick to my stomach when I went home that evening. I realized I had blown it and that the market was about to crash."- Stanley Druckenmiller on his feelings the day before the 1987 crash, *The New Market Wizards*

In the previous chapters, I provided examples of how intuition can be employed in idea selection. Instead of quantitative screening tools, we should use our gut instincts to determine what goes on our to-do lists. This is just one way to utilize intuition. Helpful gut feelings can be developed for virtually any decision that investors routinely make. This includes, but is not limited to, timing the sale of investments, position sizing and portfolio construction. In addition to reviewing past decisions, gut instincts can be developed through visualization exercises, or what Gary Klein describes as "pre-mortem" exercises. These mental simulations are particularly helpful in sensing danger with existing investments, and in portfolio construction. The pre-mortem is also an excellent way to leverage the intuition of others.

It is common practice for analysts to list risk factors associated with their investments, but few investors actually try to visualize failure. A pre-mortem exercise involves mental simulation of failure and then thinking of all the possible reasons for its occurrence. This may sound the same as quickly listing risk factors, but it is very different. When you mentally simulate your investment failing, you actually try to feel the pain from the loss on the investment. Starting with thinking about failure and then working backwards to mentally simulate what could have gone wrong actually creates "virtual experiences." These can lead to gut instincts that help to sense danger. For example, I currently own shares of Equinix (EQIX), which is a company that provides data center services. It is benefiting from the growth of the Internet and many other positive trends. Therefore, EQIX is benefiting from positive "momentum of the pendulum" and requires a growth investing approach. Recall from Chapter 5 that for growth stocks such as EQIX, the key is recognizing earlier than others when the momentum is broken. I conducted a pre-mortem exercise with EQIX where I visualized the stock being down 40% from its current price. I tried to understand how I would feel with this great of a loss. I also tried to work backwards to think about what could have caused such a slide. Instead of just listing risk factors, I thought about how events may unfold. I thought about how certain relatively minor events can lead to bigger changes. The mental simulation exercise has put me on alert for certain industry and company specific developments. An example of a negative development would be increased competition that pressures pricing. Other negative scenarios could involve EQIX's management making unnecessary and overly risky decisions, such as a relatively large acquisition of a very different business, or a very risky investment in an unfamiliar market. Because I have felt what loss would feel like, and have associated that feeling with certain events unfolding, I feel better prepared to sense danger. Hopefully, I will be more decisive with exiting my position when the time is right. Investors that have a better idea of what can go wrong with their investments are more in control. This empowers them to sell when others are still evaluating the unexpected development or are inappropriately adding even more risk. Moreover, I hope that these simulations will aid me to quickly recognize buying opportunities such as when traders become overly concerned about certain industry noise that does not fundamentally impact the company's earnings power or growth prospects.

Athletes have been using pre-mortem exercises for a long time. For example, in *The Power of Habit,* writer Charles Duhigg describes how Michael Phelps' goggles filled up with water during an Olympic race. Even though he swam a large portion of the race practically blind, Phelps still amazingly won and set a new world record. Phelps remained calm, because this was a scenario he had mentally prepared for. When Phelps was asked about swimming blind, he said to a reporter that "It felt like I imagined it would."[93]

For some great investors, intuition built to sense danger is actualized into physical changes. George Soros learned to recognize that something was wrong with his portfolio whenever acute back pain set in. Other investors, as exemplified by the quote from Stanley Druckenmiller at the start of this chapter, feel sick when they start to realize they are in trouble. These investors are self-aware enough to recognize that negative emotions, or their physical manifestations, such as back pain or an upset stomach, are signals. When something starts to happen that is contrary to your investment thesis or that you previously contemplated during a pre-mortem exercise, your brain produces a negative emotional response which sometimes is expressed physically. Dismissing these feelings is a mistake. Instead, investors should learn to recognize these emotions as alarm bells. I am not implying that people should just reverse course every time they have a bad feeling. Rather, bad feelings should be catalysts to logically reevaluate one's positioning. Remember: investment decisions should start with gut feelings, but should always be safeguarded with logic.

Most of us are biased towards overconfidence. Visualizing failure can offset this basic human inclination. It helps us realize if we are potentially taking too much risk by sizing positions too aggressively. If you can picture many scenarios of how you can lose half your investment, and if the pain of such loss would make you very uncomfortable taking risk on future investments, then you are very likely sizing the investment too aggressively no matter the potential upside. Certain investments can have many possible pathways for a large loss, while others have only a handful of scenarios that lead to disappointment. The pre-mortem exercise helps to flesh this out. For example, recall that I owned Apple's stock for some time after leaving the hedge fund industry. People generally buy a new phone every couple of years and phone manufacturers are constantly introducing new models. Thus, if Apple lost its position of having the most superior phone on the market, its market share would be at risk of declining relatively quickly when compared to manufacturers of products where there is less rapid innovation. I needed to take this into account when deciding how much of Apple's stock to buy. Too often, people focus on how much money they can make when they decide on the size of individual portfolio positions. In addition to the potential rewards, great investors pay special attention to the downside risks. They try to understand the probability of loss and are honest with themselves about how much pain they are willing to take on each investment.

The pre-mortem not only aids in understanding possible patterns that lead to loss, and if we are being too aggressive with position sizing, but it also helps in overall portfolio construction. Every investor has individual motivations, which should be constantly revisited and taken into account. I personally highly value my financial autonomy. I have a certain personal net worth threshold that I do not want to fall beneath. I know that if I do cross that lower limit, I will have a more difficult time taking risks with my personal money. I constantly conduct visualization exercises in which I envisage my net worth declining past my threshold amount. I work backward to think of scenarios that could cause this to happen. I then adjust my portfolio to minimize risks. Very often, these adjustments also limit the potential upside of my portfolio, but that is a tradeoff I am willing to make given my own personal motivations. For example, I recently realized that if the stock market crashed, I would be at risk of having my net worth go below my personal threshold. After conducting the pre-mortem, I decided to hedge my portfolio with some out-of-the-money put options ("crash-protection") on market indices. If the market doesn't decline meaningfully, the put options will expire worthless. Nevertheless, I will still believe I made the right decision, because it will have allowed me to sleep at night.

According to writer Sebastian Mallaby, Paul Tudor Jones spends about an hour every night conducting mental simulation exercises. He thinks about various scenarios such as the price of oil rising significantly or the Euro declining significantly. Jones tries to understand how certain events can impact his portfolio. He uses these visualization exercises to discover flaws in his portfolio and makes adjustments as needed. These mental simulations also prepare him to react to macro-economic news and changes in the market. For example, while others are scrambling to think of the implications of a new war in the Middle East, he may be already making investment decisions. He previously thought about this scenario and knows how to react. This gives Jones a slight edge over other macro traders. When multiplied over many trades and compounded over many years, this minor advantage has led to material outperformance.

Yet another benefit of the pre-mortem exercise is that it allows one to leverage the intuition of others. Many investors have difficulty with team-work. Because successful investing usually requires taking a contrarian stance, decisions made by committee meetings rarely lead to superior returns. The larger the group, the less contrarian a trade decision tends to be. Instead of making decisions by committee, organizations should focus on gathering valuable input from different members of the group that have relevant expertise. The key decision-maker for the trade should then harness this input to make better trading and investment choices. Gary Klein writes, "Each person has a different set of experiences, a different set of scars, and a different mental model to bring to this task."[94] Consequently, each person in a group may be able to think of scenarios that you may not have thought of. Asking others to help conduct a pre-mortem could lead to sensing some dangerous patterns that you may not have recognized on your own. I gave some examples of things that would alert me with respect to my investment in Equinix's stock. Talking to other experienced investors about how my investment in Equinix could fail has only expanded the list of risk factors I am constantly on the lookout for. While I still made an individual decision, talking to others has allowed me to understand the risks even better. I feel more prepared and in control, which helps me to be less susceptible to trading errors that come from feeling stressed or scared.

Chapter 15

Conclusion and Recommended Process Improvements

"We enjoy the process far more than the proceeds." – Warren
Buffett

When I set out to write this book, I had the goal of learning how to be
a better investor. I ended up realizing that superior investment
decisions start with an improved understanding of oneself. Too many
investment gurus skip this important step. They wrongly assume that
what works for them can work for anyone. They overlook the fact
that people are different. We each have different motivations,
personality traits and tolerances for ambiguity. Each of us is more or
less susceptible to certain common investing biases. Not until we
understand ourselves better, can we have a sense for what sort of
investment style will work best for us. The self-unaware investor is
playing a game that can only be won through dumb luck. He ends up
either trying to emulate someone that he cannot be like, or he does not
ever adopt a consistent investment framework. Without a consistent
approach to investing, intuition cannot be built. And without helpful
intuition, steady long term success becomes almost
impossible. Furthermore, successful investing involves taking
advantage of mistakes other people make. This is done through
empathizing with other participants in the market. The self-unaware
investor usually has a difficult time doing this. If he is not honest
with himself as to what he would do in certain situations, how can he
expect to have a great sense of what others will do? If the self-
unaware investor is lying to himself about not being emotionally
sensitive, how can he be expected to successfully sense when a CEO
of a portfolio company is being deceitful?

Unlike IQ and most of our personality traits, which are relatively fixed, our emotional intelligence can be improved with effort. In fact, we can become more self-aware and socially aware by just thinking about being so. Since it is so important for success, introspection should become a daily exercise for any investor. I highly recommend trying to keep a journal. The power of writing about one's emotions and thoughts has been shown empirically to be very beneficial. Reflecting on prior decisions is also the most direct route to building intuition. Without reflection, we do not obtain the most out of our experiences. They never turn into expertise. We also risk developing incorrect association biases if we do not objectively consider the role that luck had in our positive investment outcomes.

Every professional investor knows success comes from being aggressive with high conviction trades. Yet, almost nobody explores what conviction actually is. I believe that conviction is arrived at by first having a strong intuitive feeling regarding an investment. Certain patterns emerge that make a situation predictable. Given a familiar fact set, the master investor can cut through uncertainty. Therefore, he can take advantage of what is less apparent to most others. The master investor then uses his reasoning to safeguard his intuition. He also develops an empathetic edge with other market participants. He knows that as uncertainty declines, he will be paid for taking on risk that others were unwilling to assume. He knows what will make others buy after him. Conviction also involves foresight of what can go wrong. Consequently, the master investor senses, before others, dangerous patterns emerging. In the end, with a high conviction investment, the master investor makes more money than others when he is right and loses less money than most others when he is wrong.

If you only learn 10 things from reading this book, let it be these takeaways:

1. Investing success does NOT come from ignoring or suppressing emotion. Assuming that you have relevant expertise, disregarding intuition and empathetic feelings because they cannot be explained, is a mistake!

2. Self-awareness is the first and most important step in improving as an investor. An investment approach needs to fit with your unique set of motivations, personality traits, weaknesses and strengths. Don't try to be exactly like Warren Buffett if you are not like him!

3. Humans have certain common investing vulnerabilities, but everybody is unique in their susceptibility to them. Consider your weaknesses to be the investing biases and traps to which you are most prone.

4. Because we are constantly changing, introspection should be incorporated into the daily and weekly routines of any investor. Try writing in a trading journal every day.

5. An investing style that involves riding trends can require very different personality traits and competencies than a more contrarian investment strategy. It is important to make sure an investment's thesis matches the approach. For example, don't use valuation as the main justification for an investment in a stock that has been performing well for some time. Likewise, don't get shaken out of a highly contrarian bet just because short term business conditions are slightly worse than expected.

6. Trading success involves recognizing and taking advantage of the mistakes of others. This requires empathy.

7. Technical analysis is a tool for empathizing with the current shareholders of an investment. Investors that completely ignore stock charts are potentially missing out. However, avoid getting caught in the weeds of chart reading without

thinking about what the chart is telling you regarding how other shareholders may be feeling.

8. Management teams of the companies we invest in should be self-aware and trustworthy. They are making investments everyday with our money.

9. Intuition is not a magical sixth sense. It is based on pattern recognition. Within an overall market that can seem quite random, there are many patterns that repeat over and over again. The expert investor is good at quickly spotting these patterns developing. Fundamental analysis is very important, but good decision-making should start with intuition and should then be safeguarded with logic. Every potential investment should remind you of something that was successful where luck was not a major factor.

10. Intuition is best built through objectively reviewing prior decisions. It is important to make this a continuous process, since investing intuitions can become obsolete. Gut instincts can also be developed through mental simulation exercises. Instead of simply listing risk factors, try to visualize failure and then work backward to understand patterns that help with sensing danger. Mental simulations can also help with portfolio construction and are a useful way to leverage the intuitions of others.

What does all this mean for how an investment management firm should operate?

For some professional investors, the above takeaways may seem obvious. Nevertheless, very few investment firms operate with these principles in mind. Below, I offer thoughts on how certain business processes can be adjusted.

Recruiting

Investment firms market a specific investment style to their clients. Some are value investors that tend to be highly contrarian. Others are funds that utilize growth investing strategies which typically bet along with secular trends. They also market their expected investment horizons. Some are short term traders while others are very long term investors. Because we know that particular personality traits fit with specific investing styles, it should be obvious that recruiting processes weed out candidates with incompatible personalities. This can easily be done using personality tests, many of which can be found for free on the Internet. Very few firms objectively think about personality traits when hiring. Instead, most overvalue academic pedigree and IQ. They conduct interviews to simply assess likability. A candidate can be smart and personable, but if she is impulsive, she will likely not be successful in a firm that only takes a few concentrated, highly contrarian bets every year. Similarly, a new hire that is emotionally sensitive may have difficulty working at a firm that does not employ stop-losses. Firms need to think about the personality traits that fit best with their given styles, and actively recruit people that have those qualities. One way to understand which qualities are best is to make everyone already employed by the firm take a personality test. The leaders of the firm can then analyze which characteristics are common among the top performers. Moreover, firms should place an emphasis on recruiting people with high emotional intelligence. Again, tests for self-awareness and social awareness can be found on the Internet. Research has shown that people become more socially aware when they are around others who are emotionally intelligent. Therefore, recruiting with emotional intelligence in mind not only improves the chances of recruiting the right people for the right job, but it also can be a factor in making everyone else a better decision-maker. Finally, a candidate's motivation should be considered. It is generally better to look for candidates that are motivated by something other than compensation. Many people are motivated by the chance to become an expert. These are the type of people I would prefer working with since they are the most likely to learn from mistakes. Firms also need to make sure that their candidates enjoy investing for reasons that are consistent with the firm's investment horizon. For example, Lone Pine Capital has a much longer investment horizon when compared to other funds with a growth approach. This is because its leadership generally enjoys developing views regarding longer term secular trends. Therefore, Lone Pine should look for candidates that have similar motivations. People that are interested much more in investor psychology are unlikely to be successful as analysts at Lone Pine.

Leadership

A firm's overall mood fluctuates in correlation to how well or badly it is performing. When a firm is doing well, people will be happier and will ordinarily take on more risk. Because markets tend to follow boom and bust patterns, this is usually the opposite of what they should be doing. Leaders should take advantage of their influence to actively regulate mood swings. Leaders should proactively lift spirits after losses and be more morose when business is going well. They should put the focus on mistakes during the good times, and on what is being done well during the bad times. Most CEOs and CIOs do the exact opposite. They usually make employees feel even worse than they already do for losses, and they overly praise employees for good decisions. Instead of regulating mood, they amplify it.

Prioritization of Work

Successful investing starts with recognizing a familiar pattern. Before doing any work, an investment idea should remind an experienced investor of something that was successful. Then, a fair portion of the analysis should revolve around fleshing out the differences and similarities. Looking in the right places is one of the most important ways to succeed. Nevertheless, most investment firms rely on their junior analysts, people with the least intuition, to choose what to work on. This is an example of how intuition is often taken for granted. Experienced investors regularly assume that others can spot patterns emerging as well as they can. In order for intuition to be best harnessed, a firm's to-do list should come from the top down instead of from the bottom up. The majority of investment ideas that get on the to-do list should come from senior members of the organization. The firm's pipeline of work should also be actively managed. Leaders should emphasize stopping work on ideas that are unlikely to ever be high conviction trades, so that the organization's time can be better spent elsewhere. Quickly realizing that an initial gut feeling is wrong is also a skill that an experienced investor develops over time.

Position Sizing and Getting Out Of Mistakes

Too many firms overly rely on junior analysts for position sizing recommendations. Like idea selection, position sizing and sensing danger are heavily dependent on intuition. Therefore, it is nonsensical to have faith in recommendations from those in the firm that have the least intuition. This is another example of how intuition can be taken for granted. Moreover, mistakes can often be noticed more easily by the people who do not make them. It should be up to the leader, once in a while, to recognize when someone else is stuck and take action.

Conducting Group Meetings

Investment firms should reflect on what they want to achieve with meetings. It is my opinion that investing by committee does not work effectively. First, it is usually difficult for a large group to be comfortable with contrarian investments. Second, trying to get a committee on board with a decision inevitably turns the focus towards factors that are easily quantifiable and describable. Important gut feelings and empathetic realizations may be abandoned, because they are often challenging to communicate. Third, it is tough to react quickly to new information when various approvals are required. The key decisions for an investment should be made by just one or two people. However, it can still be very helpful to have meetings. Instead of being used to generate consensus, meetings should be conducted to help key decision-makers. The investor should use others as sounding boards. Meetings can be a check on potentially growing overconfident in an idea. Group discussions also allow for leveraging the intuition of others. Everyone has a different set of failures. Colleagues can help you think about scenarios that lead to loss that you may not have thought about. According to Daniel Kahneman, "the standard practice of open discussion gives too much weight to the opinions of those who speak early and assertively, causing others to line up behind them."[95] One way to compensate for this is to ask each member of the group to write down their opinions and thoughts before asking them to speak. If possible, this should be done before a meeting even takes place. Finally, group discussions can be useful to review prior choices. Instead of just calling decisions bad or good, it is important for the group to focus on why they were made. Only then can intuition successfully be built for everyone involved.

Detailed Memos for Investment Decisions

When you learn to drive a car, you think about every step. You think about turning the lights on. You think about how much pressure to apply on the gas. You think about looking into the rear view mirror once in a while. After sometime, all these actions become intuitive. For the expert, thinking too much and not acting naturally can actually be worse. Similarly, detailed investment memos are most helpful for junior analysts. They help them develop intuition. Investment memos can also help more experienced investors conduct the analysis needed to safeguard their intuition. However, investment firms should always remember that good investment decisions start with gut feelings. It can be dangerous for highly experienced investors to only focus on what is measurable. That risks ignoring their intuition. Moreover, while risk factors should be described in the memo, that is not a substitute for visualizing failure and for working backward to understand its potential causes. Finally, investment memos and other communications should be done in such a way that it is easy to objectively revisit how a decision was made and what could have been done better. For example, if a negative development causes you to sell an investment for a loss, you should be able to go back to the investment write-up to see if you considered the development occurring. If not, why not? Knowing the answer helps build the intuition to better assess risks with future investments.

Constant Evolution

The best investment firms know that gut instincts have obsolescence risk. Others in the market eventually start recognizing the same patterns that allow you to make money. Consequently, the best funds have a culture to regularly build new intuitions. They are also on the lookout for obsolescence. They don't continue doing the same thing that brought them success once it no longer works. Constant evolution can only occur through relentless review of prior decisions. Losses should be viewed as the cost of learning something new. Losses on investment decisions that are very similar to prior successful choices should be a red flag for possible obsolescence.

Portfolio Monitoring

Investments that are highly contrarian should be treated very differently than those positions that are riding a trend. Therefore, it is imperative to group the portfolio into at least these two buckets. Don't make the same mistake Julian Robertson made with US Airways. Recall how he continued to treat US Airways as a contrarian type investment even after it went up over 400%. Instead of selling after the first sign of trouble, he added to his already oversized position. It is important to be aware of when an investment moves from being highly contrarian to one that is riding a trend. Looking at the chart can help with determining to which bucket a position should belong.

Using Junior Analysts

Intuition is what drives success, and only those who have adequate experience have a chance of having helpful gut instincts. Nevertheless, junior analysts are still helpful in safeguarding intuition. They can perform fundamental analysis, build financial models and conduct other research to reduce uncertainty in an investment. In doing so, they should focus on building their own intuition. A problem is that most young people entering the investment management industry are more focused on compensation than learning. This makes no sense given the income inequality in the industry. Instead of taking the job that pays the best, they should go to firms that have an investment style that matches their personality traits. Instead of bickering over a couple of thousand dollars at bonus time, junior analysts should focus on building relationships with their mentors. They should actively review decisions made by their superiors. Finally, they should work on improving their own emotional intelligence.

Working Environment

Self-reflection, empathy and building intuition all require quiet thinking time. Therefore, it is important to create an environment that is conducive to this. Most firms operate in a manner that assumes people have an unlimited capacity to digest information. Employees are expected to respond to emails and instant messages immediately even if they are talking on the phone. Most financial analysts constantly stare at moving numbers on a Bloomberg or Routers screen even if they are not short term traders. On top of all this, firms usually have the TV tuned into CNBC, Bloomberg News or other channels. When I ask most professional investors when they are most productive, they usually talk about the weekends. For most, it is the only time when they can just sit and think. It should not be this way. Investment firms should make an effort to reduce distractions so that employees can also be very productive in building intuition during the weekdays. Lack of quiet thinking time to review prior decisions produces employees that do not translate experience into intuition. No time for mental simulations causes investors to be unprepared. Without being prepared for various scenarios, investors can feel controlled by the market and by random events rather than being in control. Consequently, they are more inclined to sell when they should actually be buying, or vice-versa. Instead of taking advantage of the mistakes of others, they are the ones making errors.

Firms should also have a cultural focus on stress reduction. This seems obvious given the negative impact that stress can have on optimal decision-making. Yet, most firms celebrate it when their employees regularly pull all-nighters or skip meals to stay glued to their monitors. Many firms also do not encourage exercise or office chitchat that reduces stress.

Portfolio Construction

Visualizing failure of the total portfolio can be just as helpful as doing so with individual investment ideas. Mental simulations of macro-economic variables help to determine where the portfolio is potentially overexposed and help to determine the bets you are really making. For example, by thinking about your portfolio's performance if interest rates rise, you may realize that your individual positions add up to a bet on a factor that you have no strong view on. Furthermore, if you do have a strong view on a macro-economic variable, mental simulation can help determine if you are actually expressing that view with the portfolio. Like pre-mortem exercises for individual investment decisions, mental simulation exercises concerning the overall portfolio can be done in such a way that leverages the intuition of others.

Evaluating Performance and Compensation

It is important to always put the focus on the decision-making process rather than on outcome. Given the role of randomness, focusing on outcomes can lead to building flawed intuitions. In order to build helpful gut instincts, analysts and portfolio managers need to do their best to be objective as to the role luck played in their winners. Moreover, a losing trade can have a good process if it is sold quickly after negative developments emerge that impact the investment's thesis. When thinking about compensation for junior members of the firm, leaders should consider motivations. Even in the investment industry, people are motivated by more than just money. For example, some people value a certain level of increased autonomy. They may prefer making less money for the freedom to work on their own schedule and with less oversight. Another example is that some people are motivated by being part of a group. They may be fine with getting paid less during good years if it also means that they are taken care of if the firm has a bad year.

What does this all mean for the individual investor?

While the government has tried to level the playing field for individual investors by introducing legislation like the Fair Disclosure Act, the professional investor still has many distinct advantages. First, institutional investors get to interview management teams face to face or over the phone. Because much of communication is non-verbal and because professional investors meet with management teams regularly, they will always have an informational advantage, if they have high social awareness. Second, the professional investor makes more investing decisions, and because she doesn't have another day job, she should have more time to reflect on these decisions. Therefore, she should have more chances to build helpful gut instincts than the individual who spends less time investing. Third, professional investors are constantly talking to other investors. They can more easily develop an empathetic edge. They do not have to try to guess what a large shareholder of a stock will do if a specific fundamental event happens. They can try to call the shareholder and ask.

While the playing field is not level, I think an individual investor can still be successful by sticking to the part of the field that is tilted in his favor. I will bet on a highly self-aware individual investor over a professional with low emotional intelligence any day of the week. Peter Lynch argues that people already have developed gut feelings regarding businesses they have exposure to. For example, a doctor may have intuition regarding the success of a new drug. An avid gamer may have a gut instinct regarding the popularity of a new game from Electronic Arts. A housewife may recognize the large potential for a new type of cleaning product from P&G. Of course, these gut feelings need to be safeguarded with logic. For understanding how to do that, please refer to other books like *Security Analysis* by Benjamin Graham. Like larger money managers, individual investors should look to have gut instincts drive the investment process, but they need to make sure that the intuition is related to an area that they have expertise in. It makes no sense for a housewife to invest in a biotech company if she has no knowledge of that sector. Furthermore, most professional investors ignore very small companies. This is because small investments cannot possibly move the needle when managing a large amount of money. Therefore, individual investors may have more of a level playing field with small cap companies. CEOs and CFOs of small businesses are also usually willing to speak or meet with individual investors. Another advantage a small investor has over institutional investors is the ability to get in and out quickly. Recall from Chapter 7 that in September 2011, I quickly shorted RIMM in the aftermarket after it reported earnings and started trading lower. I would never have been able to make a meaningful short position, as quickly as I did, if I was managing a very large amount of money. Finally, most professional investors are judged on short term results. Professionals are usually paid based on how they do in a given year. Many hedge funds send out weekly or monthly performance reports. They fear client redemptions if they have a bad month or quarter. They also fear missing out on a short term move and having mediocre results when everyone else is reporting strong returns. This fear compels most money management firms to be close to fully invested even when they do not have high conviction in their investments. Individual investors can take advantage of the short term bias of most institutions by having a longer term perspective. Individuals can also stay underinvested when they have low conviction. Consequently, they can ensure that their performance is primarily driven by higher probability bets on "fat pitches." In summary, no matter if you are a professional or not, it is important to try to take advantage of where the playing field is tilted in your favor. In any case, success starts with intuition, which should be safeguarded with analysis. Consistent superior returns also require a process to continuously improve one's emotional intelligence.

What does this all mean for the client of an investment fund?

The investment management industry currently has many people and whole organizations that are not self-aware. They do not recognize how much of their past success may have come from just being lucky. They also do not realize that their intuitions may have become obsolete. I talk to many professional investors that are frustrated by the fact that what "worked" in the past does not seem to be working anymore. Instead of putting in the effort to develop new intuitions, many hedge fund managers are currently using financial leverage as a crutch. Increased margin debt can mask weakening investment ability, but only to a point. As it did in 2008 for many funds, increased leverage can lead to disaster. It can amplify losses from bad decisions or unlucky random events. Clients should also not fall victim to status quo bias. They should remind themselves that good strong prior performance does not necessarily imply future success. Fund managers can appear to have great gut instincts one day, only to seem completely out of sync the next. Capital flows usually follow performance. As the fund you are invested in grows, it will have more difficulty putting all the new money to work into investments that continue to yield superior returns. Competitors are also likely to develop similar intuitions. The best investment managers are constantly evolving and developing new gut instincts. This is mainly accomplished through introspection. Therefore, clients should look for investment funds that have a good process for examining prior decisions. Finally, clients should rely on their own gut instincts regarding the trustworthiness, self-awareness and competency of the fund managers investing their money.

What does this all mean for life outside of investing?

The successful investor needs to stay humble, introspective and empathetic so as to continue being good at what he or she does. When done correctly, investing not only leads to wealth, but also to being a better human being. This book's concepts are applicable to many aspects of life. Being honest with oneself and making an action plan to deal with vulnerabilities can only be helpful. For example, while I am relatively outgoing, I sometimes still feel anxiety in certain social situations. Conducting visualization exercises before these types of events helps me to feel more prepared and in control. Before social gatherings, I sometimes try to think about what I can learn from each of the people I will meet. Events that once caused me anxiety are now get-togethers I increasingly look forward to. They are opportunities to learn. Moreover, improved social awareness only leads to more fulfilling relationships with family and friends. Finally, even professional investors make many more non-investing decisions than trading choices every day. Objectively reviewing these decisions can only help build the intuition to make the correct future judgments that lead to being a better parent, spouse, neighbor, boss, etc.

What does this all mean for me?

After writing this book, I have developed daily and weekly routines to understand myself and others better, deal with my particular vulnerabilities, prioritize my to-do list, evaluate investment opportunities, empathize with other market participants, monitor my portfolio, learn from prior decisions, leverage the intuition of others and anticipate danger with individual investments and my overall portfolio's construction. I also make sure that my investment approach fits with my personality and motivations. On top of all this, I still spend the majority of my time conducting the fundamental business analysis necessary to safeguard my gut instincts. Investing is not easy. I never had the delusion that it could be. In fact, I love investing precisely because it is so challenging. I do not know of another activity that demands such a continuous effort to improve oneself through introspection. I still make many mistakes and I still have a lot of work to do. However, I believe this journey of self-discovery has illuminated a roadmap to achieving my full potential.

Index

Notes

1 Sebastian Mallaby, *More Money Than God: Hedge Funds and the Making of a New Elite* (Penguin, 2010)

2 Garry Kasparov, *How Life Imitates Chess: Making the Right Moves – from the Board to the Boardroom* (Bloomsbury USA, Reprint Edition 2010).

3 Jane Spencer, "Lessons from the Brain Damaged Investor," *The Wall Street Journal*, July 21, 2005.

4 Jonah Lehrer, *How We Decide* (Houghton Mifflin Harcourt Co, 2009).

5 Richard L. Peterson, *Inside the Investor's Brain: The Power of Mind Over Money* (Wiley, 2007).

6 David Brooks, *The Social Animal: The Hidden Sources of Love, Character, and Achievement* (New York: Random House, 2011).

7 John Ameriks, Tanja Wranik and Peter Salovey, *Emotional Intelligence and Investing Behaviour* (Research Foundation of CFA Institute, 2009).

8 Travis Bradberry and Jean Greaves, *Emotional Intelligence 2.0* (TalentSmart 2009).

9 Brett N. Steenbarger, *The Daily Trading Coach: 101 Lessons for Becoming your own Trading Psychologist*, (Wiley, 2009).

10 Gary Klein, *The Power of Intuition: How to Use Your Gut Feelings to Make Better Decisions at Work* (Crown Business, Kindle Edition 2007).

11 Richard L. Peterson, *Inside the Investor's Brain: The Power of Mind Over Money* (Wiley, 2007).

12 Nassim N. Taleb, *Fooled by Randomness: The Hidden Role of Chance in Life and in the Markets* (Random House, 2 Updated Edition 2008)

13 Sebastian Mallaby, *More Money Than God: Hedge Funds and the Making of a New Elite* (Penguin, 2010)

[14] Warren Buffett, Speech to Columbia University Students, 1984

[15] Richard L. Peterson, *Market Psych: How to Manage Fear and Build Your Investor Identity* (Wiley, 2010).

[16] Travis Bradberry, *Self-Awareness: The Hidden Driver of Success and Satisfaction* (Perigee, 2009).

[17] Travis Bradberry and Jean Greaves, *Emotional Intelligence 2.0* (TalentSmart 2009).

[18] Richard L. Peterson, *Market Psych: How to Manage Fear and Build Your Investor Identity* (Wiley, 2010).

[19] Daniel Kahneman and Amos Tversky, "Prospect Theory: An Analysis of Decision Under Risk," *Econometrica,* Vol. 47, No. 2, 1979.

[20] Charles T. Munger, *The Psychology of Human Misjudgement,* 2005, p. 18.

[21] Curtis Faith, *Trading from Your Gut: How to Use Right Brain Instinct & Left Brain Smarts to Become a Master Trader* (FT Press 2009).

[22] Jason Zweig, *Your Money and Your Brain: How the New Science of Neuroeconomics can Help Make You Rich* (Simon & Schuster, 2007). p. 244.

[23] Gerd Gigerenzer, *Gut Feelings: The Intelligence of the Unconscious* (Penguin, 2008).

[24] Ari Kiev, *Mental Strategies of Top Traders: The Psychological Determinants of Trading Success* (Wiley, 2009).

[25] Dan Ariely, *Predictably Irrational: The Hidden Forces that Shape Our Decisions* (HarperCollins, 2009).

[26] Nassim N. Taleb, *Black Swan: The Impact of the Highly Improbable* (Random House; Reprint edition 2010).

[27] Peter Salovey, "Applied Emotional Intelligence: Regulating Emotions to Become Healthy, Wealthy, and Wise." In *Emotional Intelligence in Everyday Life:*

A Scientific Inquiry. Edited by J Ciarrochi, J.P. Forgas, and J.D. Mayer. (New York: Psychology Press 2001). p. 231-245

[28] Richard L. Peterson, *Market Psych: How to Manage Fear and Build Your Investor Identity* (Wiley, 2010).

[29] Alan C. Greenberg, *Memos from the Chairman* (Workman Publishing Company, 1996).

[30] Jonah Lehrer, *How We Decide* (Houghton Mifflin Harcourt Co, 2009).

[31] Nassim N. Taleb, *The Black Swan: The Impact of the Highly Improbable*, (Random House, 2007).

[32] Jason Zweig, *Your Money and Your Brain: How the New Science of Neuroeconomics can Help Make You Rich* (Simon & Schuster, 2007). p. 252.

[33] Dan Childs, "Retail Therapy: Does Sadness Mean Spending?", *ABC News*, February 8, 2008.

[34] Daniel Goleman, *The Brain and Emotional Intelligence*, (More than Sound, 2011).

[35] Richard L. Peterson, *Inside the Investor's Brain: The Power of Mind Over Money* (Wiley, 2007).

[36] Richard L. Peterson, *Market Psych: How to Manage Fear and Build Your Investor Identity* (Wiley, 2010).

[37] Ibid.

[38] Daniel Kahneman, *Thinking, Fast and Slow* (Farrar, Straus and Giroux, 2011).

[39] Jack D. Schwager, *Market Wizards: Interviews with Top Traders* (Marketplace Books, Original Classic Edition, 2006).

[40] Brett N. Steenbarger, *The Daily Trading Coach: 101 Lessons for Becoming your own Trading Psychologist*, (Wiley, 2009).

[41] Travis Bradberry and Jean Greaves, *Emotional Intelligence 2.0* (TalentSmart 2009).

[42] Howard Marks, *The Most Important Thing: Uncommon Sense for the Thoughtful Investor* (Columbia University Press, 2011).

[43] Jack D. Schwager, *Market Wizards: Interviews with Top Traders* (Marketplace Books, Original Classic Edition, 2006).

[44] Ibid.

[45] Bud Labitan, *The Four Filters Invention of Warren Buffett and Charlie Munger* (Acalmix, 2008).

[46]http://wealthymatters.com/2011/01/12/charlie-mungers-quotes-mungerisms/

[47] Tony Loton, *Stop Orders* (Harriman House, Kindle Edition, 2010).

[48] David Brooks, *The Social Animal: The Hidden Sources of Love, Character, and Achievement* (New York: Random House, 2011).

[49] Charles T. Munger, *The Psychology of Human Misjudgement*, 2005, p. 18.

[50] Daniel Kahneman, *Thinking, Fast and Slow* (Farrar, Straus and Giroux, 2011).

[51] Tim Murphy, "Who Gets to Marry a Billionaire?", *New York Magazine,* April 9, 2007.

[52] Richard L. Peterson, *Market Psych: How to Manage Fear and Build Your Investor Identity* (Wiley, 2010).

[53] Howard Marks, *The Most Important Thing: Uncommon Sense for the Thoughtful Investor* (Columbia University Press, 2011).

[54] Richard Smitten, *Jesse Livermore: World's Greatest Stock Trader* (Wiley, 2001).

[55] Sebastian Mallaby, *More Money Than God: Hedge Funds and the Making of a New Elite* (Penguin, 2010).

[56] Jack D. Schwager, *Market Wizards: Interviews with Top Traders* (Marketplace Books, Original Classic Edition, 2006).

[57] Sebastian Mallaby, *More Money Than God: Hedge Funds and the Making of a New Elite* (Penguin, 2010).

[58] Jack D. Schwager, *Market Wizards: Interviews with Top Traders* (Marketplace Books, Original Classic Edition, 2006).

[59] George Soros, *Open Society: Reforming Global Capitalism* (Public Affairs; 1st edition, November 2000).

[60] Gary Klein, *The Power of Intuition: How to Use Your Gut Feelings to Make Better Decisions at Work* (Crown Business, Kindle Edition 2007).

[61] Ibid.

[62] Brett N. Steenbarger, *The Daily Trading Coach: 101 Lessons for Becoming your own Trading Psychologist* (Wiley, 2009).

[63] trendroom.wordpress.com/2010/03/04/ed-seykota-quotes/

[64] Travis Bradberry and Jean Greaves, *Emotional Intelligence 2.0* (TalentSmart 2009).

[65] J. W. Pennebaker and C. K. Chung, "Expressive writing and its links to mental and physical health." *Oxford handbook of health psychology,* (New York: Oxford University Press, 2007), p. 3.

[66] Brett N. Steenbarger, *The Daily Trading Coach: 101 Lessons for Becoming your own Trading Psychologist* (Wiley, 2009).

[67] Jean M. Twenge and W. Keith Campbell, *The Narcissism Epidemic: Living in the Age of Entitlement,* (Free Press April 2009).

[68] trendroom.wordpress.com/2010/03/04/ed-seykota-quotes/

[69] Adam Smith, *The Theory of Moral Sentiments* (Boston: Wells and Lilly, 1817; repr 2007), p. 2-3.

[70] Burton G. Malkiel, *A Random Walk Down Wall Street: The Time-Tested Strategy for Successful Investing* (W.W. Norton & Company; Completely Revised and Updated edition; December 17, 2007).

[71] Andrew W. Lo and Jasmina Hasanhodzic, *The Evolution of Technical Analysis: Financial Prediction from Babylonian Tablets to Bloomberg Terminals* (Bloomberg Press, 2010).

[72] Jim Rogers, *A Gift to My Children: A Father's Lessons for Life and Investing* (Random House, 2009).

[73]http://wealthymatters.com/2011/01/12/charlie-mungers-quotes-mungerisms/

[74] Travis Bradberry and Jean Greaves, *Emotional Intelligence 2.0* (TalentSmart 2009).

[75] Jason Zweig, *Your Money and Your Brain: How the New Science of Neuroeconomics can Help Make You Rich* (Simon & Schuster, 2007). p. 24.

[76] Travis Bradberry and Jean Greaves, *Emotional Intelligence 2.0* (TalentSmart 2009).

[77] Mark McClish, *10 Easy Ways to Spot a Liar: The Best Techniques of Statement Analysis, Nonverbal Communication and Handwriting Analysis* (The Marpa Group, 2011).

[78] Ibid.

[79] Ibid.

[80] Richard Smitten, *Jesse Livermore: World's Greatest Stock Trader* (Wiley, 2001). p. 198.

[81] Malcolm Gladwell, B*link: The Power of Thinking without Thinking* (Back Bay Books, 2007).

[82] David Brooks, *The Social Animal: The Hidden Sources of Love, Character, and Achievement* (New York: Random House, 2011).

[83] Ray Dalio, *A Template for Understanding How the Economic Machine Works and How it is Reflected Now*, 2012.

<*http://www.bwater.com/Uploads/FileManager/research/how-the-economic-machine-works/a-template-for-understanding--ray-dalio-bridgewater.pdf*>

[84] Morgan Stanley Research, U.S. Equity Strategy, June 11, 2012.

[85] Peter Lynch and John Rothchild, *Learn to Earn: A Beginner's Guide to the Basics of Investing and Business* (Fireside, 1995). p. 132.

[86] Garry Kasparov, *How Life Imitates Chess: Making the Right Moves, from the Board to the Boardroom* (Bloomsbury USA; Reprint edition 2010).

[87] Ibid.

[88] Daniel Kahneman, *Thinking, Fast and Slow* (Farrar, Straus and Giroux, 2011).

[89] Malcolm Gladwell, *Outliers: The Story of Success* (Back Bay Books; Reprint edition, June 7, 2011).

[90] Garry Kasparov, *How Life Imitates Chess: Making the Right Moves, from the Board to the Boardroom* (Bloomsbury USA; Reprint edition 2010).

[91] Ari Kiev, *The Mental Strategies of Top Traders: The Psychological Determinants of Trading Success* (Wiley, 2009).

[92] Robert Berner with Susann Rutledge, "The Next Warren Buffett?", *Bloomberg BusinessWeek*, November 22, 2004.

[93] Charles Duhigg, *The Power of Habit: Why We Do What We Do in Life and Business* (Random House Audio, Audible Audio Edition, February 2012).

[94] Gary Klein, *The Power of Intuition: How to Use Your Gut Feelings to Make Better Decisions at Work* (Crown Business, Kindle Edition 2007).

[95] Daniel Kahneman, *Thinking, Fast and Slow* (Farrar, Straus and Giroux, 2011).

Printed in Great Britain
by Amazon.co.uk, Ltd.,
Marston Gate.